"THE OUTSIDER" delves into youth's challenging journey, addressing love, friendships, family dynamics, school struggles, and personal identity in a world rife with dilemmas and expectations. A poignant coming-of-age guide.

THE OUTSIDER

Coming-of-Age In This Moment

Edward D. Andrews

THE OUTSIDER

Coming-of-Age In This Moment

Edward D. Andrews

Christian Publishing House
Cambridge, Ohio

Copyright © 2017 Edward D. Andrews

All rights reserved. Except for brief quotations in articles, other publications, book reviews, and blogs, no part of this book may be reproduced in any manner without prior written permission from the publishers. For information, write, support@christianpublishers.org

Unless otherwise stated, Scripture quotations are from Updated American Standard Version (UASV) Copyright © 2022 by Christian Publishing House

THE OUTSIDER: Coming-of-Age In This Moment by Edward D. Andrews

ISBN-10: 1945757604

ISBN-13: 978-1945757600

Table of Contents

Book Description 8

Preface 10

Introduction 12

SECTION 1 Surviving Sexual Desires and Love 14

    THE OUTSIDER 1 Is There Anything Wrong with Flirting 15

    THE OUTSIDER 2 The Pornography Deception 19

    THE OUTSIDER 3 Peer Pressure to Have Sexual Relations 22

    THE OUTSIDER 4 Coping with Constant Sexual Thoughts? 25

    THE OUTSIDER 5 Fully Understanding the Consequences of Sexting 28

    THE OUTSIDER 6 Is Oral Sex Really Sex? 32

    THE OUTSIDER 7 Struggling with Same-Sex Attraction 36

    THE OUTSIDER 8 Is Homosexuality Truly Wrong? 40

    THE OUTSIDER 9 Making My Beliefs About Sex Known as a Protection 44

    THE OUTSIDER 10 The Truth about Sexual Assault 48

SECTION 2 Surviving My Friends 52

    THE OUTSIDER 11 Dealing with Loneliness 53

    THE OUTSIDER 12 Where Do I Fit In? 56

    THE OUTSIDER 13 Why I Struggle with Having Friends ... 59

    THE OUTSIDER 14 How Many Friends Should I have? 62

    THE OUTSIDER 15 Others Are Spreading Rumors About Me 65

    THE OUTSIDER 16 Resisting Peer Pressure to Do Wrong 68

SECTION 3 Surviving the Family 71

THE OUTSIDER 17 Viewing the House Rules in a New Light 72

THE OUTSIDER 18 Getting Along with My Brothers and Sisters 73

THE OUTSIDER 19 How Do I Find Privacy? 77

THE OUTSIDER 20 My Parents Will Not Allow Me to Do Anything 80

THE OUTSIDER 21 How Can I Cope with Heartbreak? 84

THE OUTSIDER 22 Coping with My Parent's Divorce 87

THE OUTSIDER 23 What If My Father or Mother Is Terminally Ill? 90

SECTION 4 Surviving School 94

THE OUTSIDER 24 How Do I Deal with Bullies? 95

THE OUTSIDER 25 How Can I Cope with School When I Hate It? 100

THE OUTSIDER 26 I Am Thinking of Quitting School ... 104

THE OUTSIDER 27 How Can I Improve My Grades? 107

THE OUTSIDER 28 How Can I Cope with So Much Homework? 110

THE OUTSIDER 29 How Can I Deal with Difficult Teachers? 113

SECTION 5 Surviving Who I Am 117

THE OUTSIDER 30 Why Do I Procrastinate? 118

THE OUTSIDER 31 Why Do I Focus on My Looks So Much? 122

THE OUTSIDER 32 I Feel Like Ending It All 125

THE OUTSIDER 33 Why Do I Cut Myself? 128

THE OUTSIDER 34 Are Tattoos Really that Bad? 131

THE OUTSIDER 35 Is Cursing Really That Bad? 134

THE OUTSIDER 36 Is Alcohol Really That Bad? 137

THE OUTSIDER 37 Is Anger Really That Bad?................... 140

THE OUTSIDER 38 How Can I Recover from My Mistakes? 143

SECTION 6 Surviving Recreation................................... 146

THE OUTSIDER 39 What Are the Dangers of Gaming?.. 147

THE OUTSIDER 40 Why Is My Music Choices Important? 150

THE OUTSIDER 41 How Can I Show Balance When It Comes to Sports? 153

THE OUTSIDER 42 How Is Social Media Affecting Me?. 156

SECTION 7 Surviving My Health................................... 159

THE OUTSIDER 43 How Can I Overcome My Depression? 160

THE OUTSIDER 44 How Can I Overcome My Anxiety? 163

THE OUTSIDER 45 How Can I Cope with This Constant Sadness? 166

THE OUTSIDER 46 Protecting Children from Woke Ideological Education: A Biblical Perspective 169

THE OUTSIDER 47 Help for Those Who Are Struggling with Transgender Ideology? 180

THE OUTSIDER 48 What Does the Bible Say About Transgenderism and Cross-Dressing? 187

THE OUTSIDER 49 GENDER IDENTITY: Alternative Lifestyles—Does God Approve? 193

THE OUTSIDER 50 Finding Peace Amidst Chaos: A Guide for Today's Youth... 202

Book Description

In an era of rapid change and overwhelming challenges, young individuals are often at the crossroads of identity, beliefs, and societal pressures. "THE OUTSIDER: Coming-of-Age In This Moment" offers a lifeline to the troubled souls who grapple with the adversities of modern life. Aimed specifically at the age group of 12-25, this book serves as an essential guide, shedding light on the myriad dilemmas faced by today's youth.

Divided into seven pivotal sections, the book touches on everything from the delicate nature of sexual desires and love, the challenges of maintaining genuine friendships in an age of superficiality, the complexities of family dynamics, the trials and tribulations of school life, to the deeply personal struggles of self-identity and health. Each chapter provides valuable insights grounded in Christian values and teachings, offering a conservative perspective that is both relatable and transformative.

This isn't just a book for the youth. Parents will find it a revelation, unraveling the layers of what their children are navigating in today's wicked world. It provides them with the tools to foster understanding and open channels of communication. Moreover, pastors, Christian counselors, church, and even school counselors will find it an invaluable resource, aiding them in their mission to guide the youth towards a path of righteousness and purpose.

Whether you're a teen trying to find your place in this world, a parent aiming to connect with your child, or a counselor in search of holistic approaches, "THE OUTSIDER" will provide answers, solace, and hope. It's not just about surviving these tumultuous years; it's about thriving, finding purpose, and emerging stronger, all while keeping faith at the forefront.

Equip yourself with this comprehensive guide and find the strength, understanding, and wisdom to navigate and rise above the challenges of contemporary life. For in understanding our struggles,

THE OUTSIDER

we are better placed to overcome them, leaning on faith, community, and the timeless teachings of Christ.

Preface

Navigating the intricate labyrinth of adolescence and young adulthood has never been more challenging. The echoes of a world that seems increasingly complex reverberate loudly in the ears of our youth. This complexity, combined with the traditional struggles of growing up, has necessitated a beacon to illuminate the foggy path of contemporary life. It is in this spirit that "THE OUTSIDER: Coming-of-Age In This Moment" has been crafted.

While statistics, studies, and news reports provide a macro view of what today's generation is going through, we often overlook the individual stories, the silent cries for help, and the muted celebrations of small victories. It's crucial to remember that behind every issue or challenge mentioned in this book, there's a young person trying to make sense of it all. This book seeks to bridge the widening chasm between understanding and experience, between knowledge and empathy.

In the ensuing chapters, we won't merely talk about problems or elucidate on challenges. Instead, we endeavor to offer a hand to hold, a shoulder to lean on, and a roadmap to navigate the terrain. We will explore each topic from a foundation rooted deeply in Christian values, ensuring that our compass remains directed towards Godly principles.

"THE OUTSIDER" is not a reaction to the modern world, but rather a proactive attempt to understand, empathize, and guide. It's an invitation—to understand, to be understood, and most importantly, to grow in the warmth of God's teachings amidst a world that often seems cold and indifferent.

As you turn the pages, whether you're a young person seeking direction, a parent striving for connection, or a counselor looking for deeper understanding, remember that you're not alone on this journey. Together, with faith as our guide, we can traverse the intricacies of today's world with hope, strength, and clarity.

THE OUTSIDER

Thank you for embarking on this journey with me. Let's step into the light together.

Edward D. Andrews

Author of 220+ books and Chief Translator of the Updated American Standard Version

Introduction

The cacophony of adolescence and young adulthood is amplified in today's world. With every swipe, click, and scroll, young individuals are bombarded with a deluge of information, opinions, and new challenges that can muddy the waters of their journey to maturity. It's a unique era, where the line between the digital world and reality blurs, and the pressure to fit into multiple realms grows heavier each day.

"THE OUTSIDER" seeks to be more than just a book. It aims to be a friend, a mentor, and a safe haven where genuine concerns are addressed with compassion, understanding, and wisdom. While the title may suggest feelings of isolation or detachment, it's a call to embrace individuality, to understand that in God's eyes, being an outsider is often a path to discover one's genuine self.

Each section of this book delves into critical aspects of young lives. From the ever-present struggle with self-image and identity to the external challenges posed by society, peers, and even family. But why discuss these issues under the banner of "THE OUTSIDER"? Because every teen, at some point, feels like one. And it's crucial to understand that it's okay. Feeling out of place, at odds with the world, or just plain different is not a sign of weakness. It's often the starting point of a deeper journey—a journey of self-discovery, resilience, and spiritual growth.

The Bible, our eternal guide, offers countless examples of outsiders who, with God's guidance, played pivotal roles in His divine plan. Joseph, Moses, David, Esther, and even our Savior, Jesus Christ, experienced moments when they felt out of place, misunderstood, or marginalized. Yet, with unwavering faith, they transformed their challenges into milestones of their spiritual journey.

In the digital age, where everything seems fleeting, our connection to God's Word remains a constant. Through the Scriptures, we find answers, solace, and guidance. This book, with its roots deeply embedded in Christian values, hopes to act as a conduit connecting young souls to the timeless wisdom of the Bible.

As we embark on this exploration, remember that every chapter is a testament to the fact that with faith, understanding, and perseverance, the challenges of today can be transformed into the triumphs of tomorrow. Welcome to "THE OUTSIDER." Welcome to a journey of faith, understanding, and hope in the face of modern-day challenges.

Edward D. Andrews

SECTION 1 Surviving Sexual Desires and Love

THE OUTSIDER 1 Is There Anything Wrong with Flirting

In our rapidly evolving social landscape, flirting stands at the intersection of innocence and intent, fun and potential harm. For many, especially teens who are navigating the labyrinth of emotions and social cues, flirting can seem like a harmless way to explore feelings and relationships. But is there anything inherently wrong with flirting?

Understanding Flirting

At its core, flirting is a form of communication that signals interest in another person. It's often playful, involving compliments, teasing, and subtle gestures or body language. For many teenagers, flirting can be an exciting way to express newfound feelings of attraction and to receive validation in return. It can also serve as a means to understand social dynamics and the art of communication.

The Innocent Side of Flirting

1. **Self-Discovery**: As teens grow and mature, they begin to recognize and understand their feelings of attraction towards others. Flirting can be an avenue for self-discovery, helping them discern what they're looking for in relationships.
2. **Building Social Skills**: Engaging in light and respectful banter can enhance social skills, teaching young people how to read cues, respond appropriately, and establish boundaries.
3. **Affirmation**: Positive interactions, including innocent flirting, can bolster a teen's self-esteem, affirming that they are seen and appreciated.

The Potential Pitfalls

1. **Misreading Intent**: One of the primary risks with flirting is the potential for misinterpretation. What might be a playful jest for one person could be perceived as a genuine expression of interest by another. This can lead to confusion, embarrassment, or even hurt feelings.
2. **Crossing Boundaries**: Flirting can inadvertently cross personal boundaries. While one teen might view their actions as harmless fun, another might feel uncomfortable or pressured.
3. **Fueling Gossip**: Amongst peers, especially in a school environment, flirtatious behavior can become fodder for gossip, potentially harming reputations and causing emotional distress.
4. **Diluting Genuine Feelings**: If a teen flirts indiscriminately, it might become challenging for others to gauge when their feelings are genuine. This can create difficulties in establishing authentic relationships.
5. **Leading to Unwanted Advances**: Flirting can sometimes be perceived as an open invitation for more intimate interactions. This can be dangerous, especially if the receiving end feels entitled to reciprocate with advances that weren't initially intended.

A Christian Perspective

From a Christian viewpoint, the heart's intent matters greatly. While the Bible doesn't explicitly discuss flirting, it provides principles that can guide one's conduct in interpersonal relationships.

1. **Value and Respect**: In 1 Peter 2:17, believers are encouraged to "show proper respect to everyone." This extends to interactions of a flirtatious nature. It's essential to ensure that our actions do not demean or objectify others.

2. **Guarding the Heart**: Proverbs 4:23 reminds us, "Guard your heart above all else, for it determines the course of your life." It's crucial for teens to recognize the depth of emotions and desires that flirting can stir up, ensuring they're not led astray by momentary feelings.

3. **Purity of Intent**: 1 Thessalonians 4:3-5 speaks to the importance of avoiding sexual immorality and controlling our bodies in a way that is holy and honorable. While flirting might seem distant from this, it's a gateway to deeper emotional and physical connections. Ensuring that the intent remains pure is paramount.

Navigating Flirting with Wisdom

1. **Self-awareness**: Encourage teens to understand their motivations when engaging in flirtatious behavior. Is it for fun, genuine interest, or seeking validation? Being aware can help them navigate their actions more wisely.

2. **Open Communication**: If feelings are genuine, encourage open communication rather than relying solely on flirtatious cues. This clarity can help in avoiding misunderstandings.

3. **Establish Boundaries**: It's vital for young people to establish and communicate their personal boundaries, ensuring they are not crossed inadvertently.

4. **Seek Wise Counsel**: Teens should be encouraged to discuss their feelings and actions with trusted adults or mentors. They can offer guidance, perspective, and accountability.

Flirting, while a natural part of adolescent discovery, comes with its set of challenges and considerations. By approaching it with wisdom, understanding, and a heart aligned with Scriptural principles, teens can navigate this aspect of their social world in a way that respects both themselves and others.

Why do some people do it? Some individuals engage in flirting as a means to boost their ego and seek attention. Hailey, a young woman, explains that receiving this kind of attention may lead people to desire more of it.

But if you intentionally give a false romantic impression... However, intentionally creating the impression that you have romantic interest in someone when you do not is not only callous but also questions your judgment. The Bible warns against such behavior, stating that foolishness brings joy to those who lack good sense.

What are the dangers? Flirting can harm your reputation, as it portrays insecurity and immaturity. Jeremy emphasizes that those who flirt come across as dishonest and only interested in benefiting themselves, rather than genuinely connecting with others. The Bible teaches that love does not seek its own interests.

Flirting also hurts the person being flirted with. Jacqueline shares her experience of feeling unvalued and used when encountering someone who flirts. She believes that those who engage in flirting do not genuinely care about others but are solely focused on boosting their own self-esteem. The Bible encourages seeking the advantage of others, not just our own.

Flirting can hinder genuine romance. Olivia expresses her view that a flirtatious person would be undesirable as a partner, as their behavior prevents trust and genuine connection. The psalmist David in the Bible advises against associating with those who hide their true selves.

To think about: Consider the words and actions that could potentially label you as a flirt. Reflect on how it would feel to be led to believe someone has romantic interest in you, only to discover it was not true. Avoid causing similar harm to others. Lastly, ponder the kind of person that flirts appeal to and determine if that aligns with the type of individual you wish to attract.

THE OUTSIDER 2 The Pornography Deception

In a hyper-connected digital age, young people face an unprecedented bombardment of stimuli, and few are as alluring and deceptive as pornography. To many, it offers a secretive portal to forbidden pleasure, yet this door often opens to a realm of shadows, distortions, and profound misunderstandings about human intimacy.

The Lure of the Screen

Before diving into the heart of the deception, we must first understand its appeal.

1. **Curiosity**: The adolescent years are marked by an awakening of sexual feelings and curiosity about the opposite sex.
2. **Accessibility**: Unlike previous generations, today's youth have pornographic content just a few clicks away, often free and easily accessible.
3. **Escape**: For some, it's a way to deal with stress, loneliness, or boredom.

However, what begins as an innocent curiosity or an occasional diversion can swiftly morph into a compulsive behavior with far-reaching consequences.

Understanding the Deception

1. **Distorted View of Intimacy**: Pornography presents a skewed perspective on intimacy. It reduces a profound act of love, connection, and mutual respect to a mere physical transaction. This can lead to unrealistic expectations and misunderstandings about the nature of healthy relationships.

2. **Objectification**: Porn often objectifies individuals, reducing them to mere instruments of pleasure. This dehumanization can permeate one's real-life perspective, making it challenging to see others as beings with feelings, desires, and worth beyond the physical.
3. **Impact on Self-Worth**: Regular consumption can also distort one's self image. Teens may feel pressured to conform to the unrealistic standards portrayed, leading to feelings of inadequacy.

The Spiritual Implications

From a Christian perspective, the body is considered the temple of the Holy Spirit (1 Corinthians 6:19). Engaging with pornography can be seen as defiling this temple, not just physically, but mentally and spiritually as well. It can become a barrier, distancing one from a pure relationship with God.

Physical and Psychological Effects

1. **Brain Chemistry**: Pornography can affect the brain similarly to other addictive substances. Over time, one might require more explicit material to achieve the same level of arousal, leading to a deepening spiral of consumption.
2. **Relationship Impact**: Early exposure can condition the brain to expect unrealistic scenarios in real-life relationships, leading to dissatisfaction and dysfunction.
3. **Mental Health**: Prolonged exposure can lead to feelings of guilt, shame, anxiety, and depression.

Breaking the Chains of the Deception

Recognizing the deception is the first step. However, breaking free and ensuring one doesn't fall back into the trap requires concerted effort.

1. **Accountability**: Sharing struggles with a trusted friend or mentor can be the first step towards recovery. They can offer support, understanding, and accountability.
2. **Limiting Access**: Using filters or parental controls, even for oneself, can serve as a deterrent.
3. **Replacement Activities**: Engaging in constructive activities can divert the mind from urges. This could be physical exercise, pursuing a hobby, or diving into Scripture.
4. **Professional Counseling**: For those deeply ensnared, seeking professional Christian counseling can provide tailored strategies and coping mechanisms.

Community and Church Role

The church and community play a crucial role in aiding those ensnared by this deception. Open dialogue, education about the dangers, and creating a supportive environment can make a significant difference.

1. **Open Conversations**: Creating a safe space where teens can discuss their struggles without judgment can be therapeutic.
2. **Educational Workshops**: Organizing sessions that dive deep into the repercussions of pornography can serve as a deterrent for many.

In conclusion, while the digital age presents numerous challenges, it also offers a plethora of resources to combat them. Recognizing the profound deception of pornography and taking proactive steps can ensure that young people forge relationships based on genuine intimacy, respect, and love. In doing so, they honor not only their own body and spirit but also the God who created them.

Edward D. Andrews

THE OUTSIDER 3 Peer Pressure to Have Sexual Relations

The journey from adolescence to adulthood is riddled with challenges, not the least of which is the pressure from peers to engage in sexual activity. In a world that often reduces the profound act of intimacy to a mere rite of passage, how can young believers navigate these pressures while upholding their values and convictions?

Understanding the Pressure

The World's View vs. God's Design: Today's society, influenced heavily by media and popular culture, frequently portrays premarital sex as normal and even expected. However, this perspective contrasts sharply with the biblical view of sex as a sacred bond reserved for marriage (Hebrews 13:4). To understand the pressure, it's crucial to discern the vast gulf between the world's approach and God's intention for human relationships.

The Need for Acceptance: At the heart of peer pressure is the deep-seated human desire for acceptance. During adolescence, this longing intensifies, often making the opinions of peers more influential than those of parents or other authority figures.

The Misconceptions of 'Maturity': Many young people equate sexual activity with maturity or adulthood. The thought being, "If I do this, I will be seen as grown-up."

Biblical Perspectives on Intimacy

God's design for sex is rooted in love, commitment, and unity. It's not merely a physical act but a profound expression of love between a husband and wife (Genesis 2:24). It's essential to view sex through this lens, recognizing its divine purpose and the responsibility that accompanies it.

1 Corinthians 6:18-20: Our bodies are not meant for sexual immorality but for the Lord. Engaging in premarital sex not only goes against God's design but also defiles our bodies, which are temples of the Holy Spirit.

The Consequences of Succumbing to Pressure

Physical Repercussions: Engaging in premarital sex exposes individuals to the risk of unwanted pregnancies and sexually transmitted diseases.

Emotional Toll: The emotional and psychological consequences can be profound. Feelings of guilt, shame, and regret often accompany such decisions. Moreover, when relationships built on sexual intimacy alone end, the emotional pain can be excruciating.

Spiritual Implications: Giving in to temptation can lead to a weakened spiritual state, making it harder to resist future temptations and grow in one's relationship with God.

Equipping Oneself Against the Pressure

Building a Strong Foundation in Scripture: Rooting oneself in the Word of God provides clarity and strength. Scriptures like 1 Corinthians 6:13-20 and 1 Thessalonians 4:3-5 offer guidance and reinforce the importance of sexual purity.

Seeking Wise Counsel: Engaging in open conversations with trusted elders, mentors, or pastors can provide valuable insights and support.

Accountability Partners: Having friends who share similar values can be a source of encouragement and accountability.

Setting Boundaries: Establishing clear physical and emotional boundaries in relationships can serve as safeguards.

Engaging in Wholesome Activities: Participating in church groups, sports, or other wholesome activities can redirect focus and provide a sense of purpose and community.

Dealing with Mistakes and Finding Redemption

It's crucial to remember that everyone falls short (Romans 3:23). For those who have succumbed to the pressure, there's always hope in Christ's redemptive power.

Seeking Forgiveness: Repentance and seeking God's forgiveness is the first step towards healing. Remember, God's grace is abundant, and He is faithful to forgive (1 John 1:9).

Restoring Purity: While past mistakes can't be erased, with God's help, purity can be restored. Committing to abstinence and seeking God's strength can set one on the path of redemption.

Seeking Counseling: Christian counseling can provide guidance, healing, and strategies for maintaining purity in the future.

The pressures to engage in sexual activity during one's adolescent years can be immense. Yet, by grounding oneself in the truth of Scripture, seeking community support, and focusing on God's design for intimacy, young believers can navigate these pressures with integrity. The journey might be challenging, but the rewards of honoring God with one's body and choices are eternal.

THE OUTSIDER 4 Coping with Constant Sexual Thoughts?

Sexuality is an integral part of human nature, designed by God as a beautiful expression of love and intimacy between a husband and wife. Yet, during adolescence, as the body matures and hormones surge, it is entirely normal for young people to grapple with frequent and sometimes overwhelming sexual thoughts. Navigating this tumultuous season, especially within the framework of Christian values, requires understanding, grace, and practical strategies.

Understanding the Onset of Sexual Thoughts

Biological Changes: Adolescence heralds the onset of puberty, where the body undergoes significant hormonal and physical changes. This natural process prepares the body for procreation, inevitably leading to increased sexual awareness and thoughts.

The Brain's Role: The adolescent brain is still developing, particularly the prefrontal cortex responsible for decision-making, impulse control, and understanding consequences. This developmental phase can lead to heightened impulsivity and curiosity.

Cultural Influence: We live in a hypersexualized society. Whether it's through movies, music, advertisements, or social media, young minds are consistently bombarded with sexual imagery and messages.

The Biblical Perspective: Sexuality, in its pure and intended form, is a gift from God. The Song of Solomon in the Bible is a testament to the beauty of human love and desire. Yet, God's design is for these feelings to be expressed within the commitment of marriage (Hebrews 13:4).

Strategies to Cope with Constant Sexual Thoughts

Guarding the Mind:

Scriptural Meditation: Philippians 4:8 reminds believers to think about things that are true, noble, right, pure, lovely, and admirable. Memorizing and meditating on such Scriptures can redirect the mind when it's flooded with unwanted thoughts.

Practical Application: Intentionally minimize exposure to sexually provocative media. Be selective about movies, music, and social media content. This doesn't mean living in a bubble but being discerning and cautious.

Physical Outlets: Engaging in physical activities like sports, jogging, or even simple exercises can help channel some of the pent-up energy and reduce the intensity of sexual thoughts.

Fostering Healthy Relationships: Building friendships based on mutual respect, shared interests, and spiritual growth can provide a meaningful diversion from constant sexual preoccupation.

Seeking Accountability: Having a trusted individual, be it a youth leader, mentor, or close friend, who can be a confidant and an accountability partner can be invaluable. Sharing struggles and seeking advice can provide relief and practical wisdom.

Engaging in Prayer: Regular, heartfelt prayer is a powerful tool. By laying out one's feelings, vulnerabilities, and temptations before God, one can seek His strength and guidance. Remember the promise in 1 Corinthians 10:13, that God will not let you be tempted beyond what you can bear.

Avoiding Isolation: Loneliness can amplify sexual thoughts and lead to temptations like pornography or masturbation. Engaging in group activities, church events, or community service can provide healthy distractions.

Recognizing Triggers: Being aware of what amplifies sexual thoughts can help in avoiding or dealing with them. This could be certain movies, books, places, or even conversations.

Dealing with Guilt and Shame

While it's essential to strive for purity of thought and action, it's equally crucial to understand that feeling tempted isn't a sin—yielding to it is. Everyone, even the most devout believers, grapples with temptation (Hebrews 4:15). The key lies in how one responds.

Resting in God's Grace: For those who may have acted on their sexual thoughts, it's vital to remember that God's grace is sufficient. Repentance, seeking forgiveness, and making a conscious decision to abstain from future indiscretions is the path to restoration (1 John 1:9).

Avoiding the Cycle: Repentance is not just about seeking forgiveness but also about making a determined effort to avoid the same pitfalls. Implementing the coping strategies mentioned can be helpful in this journey.

Adolescence is undeniably challenging, more so in today's world, where the line between right and wrong seems increasingly blurred. Yet, with God's word as a compass, a supportive Christian community, and practical coping mechanisms, young believers can navigate the turbulent waters of sexual thoughts, emerging stronger in their walk with Christ. Remember, in every challenge lies an opportunity for growth, reliance on God, and deepened faith.

Edward D. Andrews

THE OUTSIDER 5 Fully Understanding the Consequences of Sexting

In today's digital age, the rise of smartphones and instant messaging apps has revolutionized how adolescents communicate. One alarming trend that has emerged, particularly among teenagers, is "sexting"—the act of sending or receiving sexually explicit texts, images, or videos. While it might seem like a harmless act of flirtation or a way of exploring one's sexuality, the consequences of sexting, both immediate and long-term, are profound. Let's delve into understanding these repercussions from a moral, psychological, legal, and spiritual perspective.

The Immediate Consequences of Sexting

Emotional and Psychological Impact:

- **Embarrassment and Regret**: Once a private image or message is out there, it's nearly impossible to retract. The immediate realization of this can lead to feelings of regret and deep embarrassment.
- **Objectification**: The person in the explicit content is often reduced to an object of desire rather than being seen for their entire personhood.
- **Risk of Bullying and Harassment**: Content can be used as blackmail or be shared without consent, leading to cyberbullying or even real-world harassment.

Legal Repercussions:

- **Child Pornography Charges**: In many jurisdictions, creating, distributing, or possessing explicit content of a minor, even if it's a selfie, can be categorized as child pornography. This can lead to severe legal consequences, including registration as a sex offender.
- **Cyberbullying Laws**: Sharing someone else's intimate photos or messages without their consent may also fall under cyberbullying laws in certain jurisdictions.

Potential for Exploitation:

- **Falling into Wrong Hands**: There's always a risk that content might be accessed by predatory individuals, leading to potential exploitation or blackmail.

The Long-Term Implications of Sexting

Digital Footprint:

- **Indelibility of Online Content**: The digital realm rarely forgets. Once content is uploaded or shared, it can be replicated, stored, or redistributed countless times, making it nearly impossible to erase entirely.
- **Future Repercussions**: Explicit content can resurface years later, impacting job opportunities, relationships, and one's public image.

Relational Consequences:

- **Trust Issues**: Engaging in sexting can create mistrust in future relationships, with partners worrying about discretion and past actions.
- **Distorted View of Intimacy**: Regular sexting can lead to a distorted view of what genuine intimacy and relationships entail.

Spiritual Implications:

- **Violation of Biblical Principles**: Scripture upholds the values of modesty, purity, and respecting the sanctity of one's body. Sexting can be seen as a violation of these values (1 Corinthians 6:19-20).
- **Guilt and Spiritual Struggle**: Engaging in actions that conflict with one's religious beliefs can lead to feelings of guilt, spiritual turmoil, and distancing from one's faith community.

Navigating the Pressure to Sext

In a world that increasingly normalizes the sharing of explicit content, it's essential for young individuals to be equipped with the knowledge and conviction to navigate these pressures.

Open Communication:

- **Finding Trusted Individuals**: Encourage teens to have open conversations with trusted adults about their feelings, pressures, and doubts related to sexting.

Education:

- **Awareness of Legal Consequences**: Being informed about the potential legal consequences can deter many from engaging in risky behaviors.
- **Understanding the Permanence**: Emphasizing the lasting nature of digital content can be a wake-up call.

Spiritual Guidance:

- **Revisiting Biblical Values**: Regularly engaging with Scripture, especially verses that underscore the importance of purity, can act as a moral compass (1 Thessalonians 4:3-5).
- **Prayer and Reflection**: Encouraging a habit of prayer and spiritual reflection can help teens seek divine guidance in moments of temptation.

Healing and Restoration for Those Who've Sexted

It's crucial to approach individuals who've engaged in sexting with empathy and understanding, recognizing the immense societal pressures they face.

Seeking Forgiveness: Engaging in genuine repentance and seeking God's forgiveness is the first step towards healing (1 John 1:9).

Restorative Conversations: Speaking with affected parties and seeking reconciliation can be therapeutic and mend broken relationships.

Professional Counseling: For those deeply affected by the repercussions of sexting, professional Christian counseling can provide healing, coping strategies, and a way forward.

Conclusion

In an age where digital communication is the norm, sexting poses a significant challenge, especially for impressionable teens. By understanding its grave consequences and armed with a spiritual and moral framework, young Christians can make informed choices, honoring both their bodies and their faith.

Edward D. Andrews

THE OUTSIDER 6 Is Oral Sex Really Sex?

Sexuality is a complex and multi-faceted part of human nature. As young individuals navigate their formative years, questions about various intimate acts inevitably arise. One such query, often imbued with both curiosity and uncertainty, is: "Is oral sex really sex?" To unpack this question, we will approach it from various angles, considering its physical, emotional, moral, and spiritual implications.

The Physical Definition

Understanding the Act:

- **Oral Sex Defined**: At its most basic, oral sex involves using the mouth, lips, or tongue to stimulate a partner's genitalia.

Medical Perspective:

- **Sexual Transmission**: Just as with penetrative sex, oral sex can lead to the transmission of sexually transmitted infections (STIs) if precautions aren't taken. Diseases like herpes, gonorrhea, and syphilis can be passed through this act.

The Emotional Dimension

Intimacy and Vulnerability:

- **A Personal Act**: Oral sex, much like any other intimate act, requires vulnerability. Partners are revealing a very private part of themselves, both literally and figuratively.
- **Bonding and Connection**: Physiologically, engaging in intimate acts releases chemicals like oxytocin, often termed the "bonding hormone." This hormone can create feelings of closeness and attachment.

The Moral Perspective

Cultural Views:

- **Fluid Definitions**: Modern culture often presents a spectrum of views on what "sex" entails. Some see oral sex as a less intimate act than penetrative sex, while others view them on par in terms of intimacy and commitment.

Christian Ethics:

- **Sexual Purity**: From a conservative Christian standpoint, the act of sexual intimacy is reserved for marriage (Hebrews 13:4). Any intimate act that evokes sexual passion, including oral sex, is viewed under this lens.
- **Avoiding Temptation**: Engaging in oral sex can often lead to further sexual acts, which can be a stumbling block for those wishing to abstain until marriage (1 Corinthians 6:18).

The Spiritual Dimension

God's Design for Sexuality:

- **A Gift for Marriage**: In the Christian worldview, sex is not merely a physical act. It's a spiritual and emotional connection between two individuals, symbolizing the union of Christ and the Church (Ephesians 5:31-32). Thus, any sexual act, including oral sex, is to be approached with this sanctity in mind.
- **Guarding One's Heart**: The Bible often emphasizes the importance of guarding one's heart and maintaining purity in thought and action (Proverbs 4:23). Engaging in intimate acts outside the covenant of marriage can pose challenges to one's spiritual wellbeing.

Navigating Peer Pressure and Modern Norms

Today's young individuals often face immense pressure from peers and the broader culture, promoting a more casual approach to intimacy.

Finding Clarity:

- **Biblical Standards**: Grounding oneself in Scripture provides clarity. The Bible may not specifically mention oral sex, but its principles on sexual purity and integrity are clear.
- **Seeking Counsel**: Engaging in open dialogue with trusted spiritual mentors, parents, or Christian counselors can help individuals navigate their feelings and questions around this topic.

A Path Forward for the Troubled and Curious

Seeking Forgiveness and Grace:

- **God's Mercies Are New Every Morning**: For those who feel they've made mistakes, it's essential to remember that God's grace and forgiveness are ever-present (Lamentations 3:22-23).
- **Reaffirming Commitments**: Young individuals can always choose to recommit themselves to purity and seek God's guidance in their sexual choices.

Open Conversations:

- **Safe Spaces**: Create environments where teens and young adults can express their doubts, questions, and curiosities without judgment.
- **Informed Choices**: Equip them with the knowledge and spiritual tools to make informed decisions about their bodies and relationships.

Understanding God's Standards on Sexual Morality

The Bible provides guidance on sexual morality, emphasizing the importance of abstaining from sexual immorality to align with God's will (1 Thessalonians 4:3). The term "sexual immorality" encompasses all forms of intimate conduct outside of marriage, including intercourse, oral sex, anal sex, and masturbating another person. Engaging in sexual immorality not only has serious consequences but can also damage one's relationship with God (1 Peter 3:12).

The Consequences of Sexual Immorality

According to the Bible, practicing sexual immorality is considered sinning against one's own body (1 Corinthians 6:18). It highlights that such behavior can have physical, spiritual, and emotional repercussions. Even oral sex can lead to harmful consequences, causing individuals to feel used, regretful, or vulnerable, just as with vaginal sex (Talking Sex With Your Kids).

God's Laws as Beneficial Guidance

The Bible states that God, as our Creator, teaches us to benefit ourselves (Isaiah 48:17). It encourages us to consider whether we believe God's laws regarding sex truly benefit us or restrict us. An analogy can be drawn to a busy highway with speed limits, traffic signals, and stop signs. Do we see these regulations as restrictions or protections? Ignoring them would lead to chaos and potential harm.

Reaping What You Sow

Similar to traffic regulations, God's standards on sexual morality are meant to guide us towards a fulfilling and morally upright life. Ignoring these standards has consequences, as the Bible warns that we will reap what we sow (Galatians 6:7). The book Sex Smart notes that abandoning our beliefs and engaging in activities that go against our values erodes self-respect. Conversely, living in accordance with God's standards not only demonstrates true moral character but also allows us to maintain a clean conscience (1 Peter 3:16).

By understanding and adhering to God's principles on sexual morality, we can navigate our relationships and choices with wisdom, respecting ourselves and striving for moral integrity.

Edward D. Andrews

THE OUTSIDER 7 Struggling with Same-Sex Attraction

Navigating the adolescent and young adult years is intrinsically challenging. But when young individuals find themselves grappling with feelings and attractions that seem contrary to their faith or the beliefs of their community, the journey can become intensely more complicated. One such struggle that many face is with same-sex attraction. This chapter seeks to shed light on this struggle from a conservative Christian perspective, acknowledging the reality of the feelings while providing guidance grounded in faith.

Understanding Same-Sex Attraction

- **A Definition**: At its core, same-sex attraction refers to emotional, physical, or romantic attraction to someone of the same gender.
- **It's Real**: It's crucial to recognize and affirm that these feelings are genuine and can be deeply ingrained in an individual's psyche.

The Biblical Stance

Creation and Intent:

- **God's Design**: The conservative Christian view holds that God designed male and female to complement each other in a marital relationship (Genesis 2:24). This design is intended to reflect the covenantal love between Christ and the Church.
- **Scriptural References**: Various passages in the Bible are often cited in discussions on homosexuality, such as Leviticus 18:22, Romans 1:26-27, and 1 Corinthians 6:9-10. These texts, from a conservative standpoint, describe same-sex acts as contrary to God's design.

The Emotional and Psychological Aspect

The Weight of the Struggle:

- **Internal Conflict**: Young individuals experiencing same-sex attraction may wrestle with guilt, shame, or confusion, especially if their feelings seem at odds with their faith.
- **The Loneliness**: Many feel isolated, fearing rejection if they open up about their struggles.

The Broader Cultural Perspective

The Changing Tide:

- **Societal Acceptance**: Today's culture largely promotes acceptance and affirmation of various sexual orientations. This can further intensify the internal conflict young Christians with same-sex attraction might feel.
- **Navigating the Middle Ground**: Balancing one's faith with societal expectations and personal feelings can feel like walking a tightrope.

Seeking Guidance and Support

Spiritual Counsel:

- **Pastoral Guidance**: Engaging in open dialogue with trusted spiritual mentors or Christian counselors can provide clarity and support.
- **Scriptural Mediation**: Immersing oneself in Scripture, not just the passages on sexuality but those on God's grace, love, and mercy, can bring comfort.

Community and Acceptance:

- **Finding Safe Spaces**: It's essential for young people to find safe environments where they can express their feelings, doubts, and curiosities without judgment.
- **The Role of Christian Community**: Churches and Christian groups have a unique opportunity (and responsibility) to approach individuals with compassion, offering support without compromising on doctrine.

Choosing a Path Forward

Personal Convictions:

- **Aligning Actions with Beliefs**: For some, the choice to live in celibacy or seek heterosexual relationships stems from a desire to align their actions with their faith convictions.
- **Continued Prayer and Reflection**: Consistent prayer and self-reflection can guide individuals in making decisions that feel right for their spiritual journey.

The Role of Therapy:

- **Ethical Therapy**: It's essential to seek therapeutic methods that respect the individual's faith and beliefs. "Conversion therapy" has been widely discredited and can be harmful. Instead, counseling should focus on helping individuals navigate their feelings within the framework of their faith.

Hope, Grace, and Identity

Our Identity in Christ:

- **Beyond Sexual Orientation**: While sexuality is a significant part of human experience, it's not the sum of one's identity. The primary identity of a believer lies in being a child of God, redeemed and loved (Galatians 3:26).
- **God's Unchanging Love**: Regardless of struggles or feelings, God's love remains constant. His grace extends to all, and His mercies are new every morning (Lamentations 3:22-23).

Understanding Same-Sex Attraction: What Does It Mean?

Is It Just a Phase?

It's essential to understand that in numerous instances, same-sex attraction can be a fleeting experience.

Consider the experience of Lisette, 16, who once felt an attraction towards a female peer. She reflects, "My biology classes taught me that during our adolescent years, there's a significant fluctuation in hormone levels. I genuinely believe that if more young individuals had this knowledge about their bodies, they might see that same-sex attractions can be transitory and wouldn't necessarily feel labeled or pressured into identifying as gay."

Making Informed Choices

Young individuals face a significant decision—either to embrace society's ever-changing perspectives on sexuality or to adhere to the more timeless, principled guidelines provided in sacred scriptures.

But what happens if one's same-sex attractions seem persistent, not just a momentary feeling? Is it unjust or unkind for religious teachings to advise against pursuing homosexual relationships?

If you're pondering the above, it's essential to recognize that the underlying premise is the belief that humans are inevitably driven by their sexual desires. However, sacred texts like the Bible elevate human potential, indicating that individuals have the capacity to exercise restraint over unwarranted sexual impulses. —Colossians 3:5.

This perspective is not unduly strict. It essentially guides those experiencing homosexual desires to follow the same principle applied to those with heterosexual attractions, which is to "flee from fornication." (1 Corinthians 6:18). The truth remains that countless individuals, wanting to align with these spiritual standards, exercise self-discipline in the face of various temptations. Similarly, those with homosexual feelings can exercise the same restraint, especially if their primary desire is to align with divine principles.—Deuteronomy 30:19.

The struggle with same-sex attraction, especially within a conservative Christian context, is profound. However, with understanding, guidance, and an unwavering focus on God's love and grace, young individuals can navigate this journey, knowing they are never truly alone. They are continually held in the loving embrace of a God who sees the depths of their hearts and loves them unconditionally.

Edward D. Andrews

THE OUTSIDER 8 Is Homosexuality Truly Wrong?

Homosexuality has been one of the most debated topics within Christian circles for decades. With increasing societal acceptance and advocacy for LGBTQ+ rights, young Christians often grapple with reconciling their beliefs and the shifting cultural landscape. The question that often arises is: Is homosexuality truly wrong according to the Bible?

A Historical Perspective

Ancient Context:

- **Cultural Practices**: Homosexuality, especially in ancient Greece and Rome, was practiced differently than in modern western societies. Understanding this context is crucial when examining biblical texts on the subject.

The Biblical Stance

Old Testament References:

- **Leviticus:** The Old Testament, in Leviticus 18:22 and 20:13, explicitly describes same-sex acts among men as an "abomination." However, it's essential to note that Levitical law also had many other stipulations, some of which are not adhered to by Christians today.

New Testament References:

- **Romans 1:26-27**: Paul, in his letter to the Romans, mentions same-sex acts as unnatural. However, the broader context of

this passage speaks against idolatry and people turning away from God.
- **1 Corinthians 6:9-11 and 1 Timothy 1:10**: Paul includes "men who practice homosexuality" among those who will not inherit the kingdom of God. Still, he also lists other sins, reminding us of the broader context of human imperfection.

The Broader Theological Perspective

- **Original Design**: Some theologians argue that God's original design for sexual relationships was between a man and a woman, based on Genesis 2:24.
- **The Nature of Sin**: From a conservative Christian perspective, all humans are sinners, with none righteous (Romans 3:10). Thus, singling out one particular sin can be seen as incongruent with the broader Christian message of redemption and grace.

Emotional and Relational Considerations

Innate Feelings:
- **Understanding Orientation**: It's crucial to distinguish between same-sex attraction (an innate feeling) and acting upon that attraction. Many believe the attraction itself is not sinful, but acting upon it is.

Relationships and Love:
- **More Than Sex**: Relationships are multifaceted, comprising emotional, spiritual, and physical connections. Recognizing this complexity ensures a more comprehensive understanding of the issue.

The Modern Church and Homosexuality

Varied Views:

- **Conservative Views**: Many conservative denominations and theologians hold to the belief that acting upon homosexual feelings is sinful based on their interpretation of Scripture.
- **Progressive Views**: Some modern Christian denominations and theologians believe that committed same-sex relationships can be blessed by God and that the biblical prohibitions were addressing different contexts, like temple prostitution or pederasty. This of course is biblically wrong. 1 Corinthians 6:9 says, "Or do you not know that the unrighteous will not inherit the kingdom of God? Do not be deceived; neither fornicators, nor idolaters, nor adulterers, nor men of passive homosexual acts, nor men of active homosexual acts." The two Greek terms refer to passive men partners and active men partners in consensual homosexual acts. "nor men of passive homosexual acts [μαλακοὶ], nor men of active homosexual acts [ἀρσενοκοῖται]"

Navigating Personal Convictions

- **Scripture and Prayer**: Engaging deeply with Scripture, underpinned by fervent prayer, can help individuals form personal convictions.
- **Seeking Guidance**: Dialogue with trusted spiritual mentors, pastors, or Christian counselors can be invaluable for those navigating this complex issue.

Love, Acceptance, and the Conservative Stance

Bridging the Gap:

- **Love and Judgment**: While maintaining a conservative view on homosexuality, it's crucial for Christians to approach individuals with genuine love, compassion, and understanding, following Jesus' example of love without condoning what they believe to be sin.
- **The Call to Holiness**: All Christians are called to a life of holiness, which encompasses far more than one's sexual behavior.

The Struggle for Young Christians

Acceptance and Belief:

- **The Inner Turmoil**: For young Christians experiencing same-sex attraction or questioning their sexuality, reconciling their feelings with their faith can be profoundly challenging.
- **Community and Acceptance**: Finding supportive Christian communities, which can hold to conservative values while offering genuine love and understanding, can be crucial for young believers.

Conclusion

The topic of homosexuality within Christianity is multifaceted and deeply personal. For young Christians navigating this issue, it's essential to ground oneself in Scripture, prayer, and open dialogue. Regardless of one's stance on homosexuality, the overarching message of the Gospel—God's love, grace, and redemption—is available to all.

Edward D. Andrews

THE OUTSIDER 9 Making My Beliefs About Sex Known as a Protection

In a world saturated with varying sexual ideologies and a myriad of pressures, young people often find themselves at a crossroads. Within the conservative Christian framework, there's a call to holiness and purity. Thus, it's essential, especially in these formative years, to be proactive about understanding and expressing one's beliefs about sex. This isn't just a matter of religious adherence—it can serve as a genuine form of protection.

Understanding Sexual Purity from a Biblical Perspective

God's Design for Sex:

- **Sacredness of the Act**: The Bible describes sex as a union between a man and a woman, an act of becoming "one flesh" (Genesis 2:24). It is a divine gift meant to express love and procreation within the bounds of marriage.

- **Maintaining Purity**: In 1 Thessalonians 4:3-5, Paul exhorts believers to avoid sexual immorality, controlling their bodies in holiness and honor.

The Protective Power of Speaking Out

Clear Boundaries:

- **Defining Limits**: Being upfront about one's beliefs establishes clear boundaries. When others know where you

stand, it becomes easier to navigate relationships and prevent potential missteps.
- **Reduced Peer Pressure**: Speaking out about one's convictions can reduce the intensity of peer pressure. When peers understand a person's strong convictions, they are less likely to persuade them to compromise.

Building Confidence in One's Convictions:

- **Affirming Faith**: The act of speaking out strengthens and affirms personal faith. It solidifies convictions and brings them to the forefront of one's mind.
- **Developing Integrity**: By aligning one's words with actions, young people develop a sense of integrity. This wholeness in thought and action can serve as a shield against temptations.

The Social Implications of Speaking Out

Navigating Relationships:

- **Choosing Like-minded Friends**: By expressing beliefs, young Christians can attract friendships with those who share similar convictions, providing mutual encouragement.
- **Dating and Courtship**: In romantic relationships, making beliefs clear from the outset can prevent misunderstandings and heartaches. It ensures both partners are on the same page about boundaries and expectations.

Potential Pushback and Perseverance:

- **Facing Opposition:** Young people should be prepared to face opposition or ridicule from some peers. However, holding firm to beliefs can lead to deepened faith and resilience.
- **Counting the Cost:** Jesus spoke about counting the cost of discipleship (Luke 14:28). Similarly, young believers must recognize that there might be social costs to standing firm in their convictions, but the eternal rewards far outweigh them.

Strategies for Making Beliefs Known

Open Conversations:

- **Starting Early:** Don't wait for a heated moment or pressure situation. Begin conversations about beliefs and boundaries early in relationships.
- **Being Specific:** Instead of vague statements, be specific about what is and isn't acceptable. This clarity can prevent confusion and potential overstepping of boundaries.

Utilizing Community Support:

- **Engaging Mentors and Leaders:** Engage in conversations with church leaders, youth mentors, and trusted elders. They can offer guidance, prayer support, and encouragement.
- **Group Settings:** Discussing sexual beliefs in group settings, such as Bible studies or youth groups, can offer a safe environment for discussion and mutual encouragement.

Scriptural Anchoring:

- **Memorize Relevant Verses**: Psalm 119:11 says, "I have hidden your word in my heart that I might not sin against you." Memorizing scriptures related to purity can be a powerful tool during moments of temptation or doubt.

- **Regular Bible Study**: Regular engagement with the Bible deepens understanding and conviction. It's essential to have a robust scriptural foundation to explain and defend one's beliefs.

In the Modern Digital Age

- **Online Presence**: In today's digital age, beliefs aren't just communicated face-to-face. Young people should be mindful of their online presence, ensuring it aligns with their convictions.

- **Avoiding Ambiguity**: Whether in text messages, social media, or other digital platforms, be clear and unambiguous about beliefs and boundaries.

Conclusion

For young believers navigating the challenges of the modern world, making their beliefs about sex known is more than just a proclamation—it's a protective measure. In the face of societal pressures and potential pitfalls, a clear declaration of one's convictions can serve as a shield. It fortifies the soul, strengthens relationships, and affirms the path of righteousness they've chosen to walk.

THE OUTSIDER 10 The Truth about Sexual Assault

Sexual assault is an issue that's often clouded in myths, misunderstanding, and secrecy, particularly in conservative circles. It's crucial for young people to have a clear understanding of what sexual assault is, the emotional and psychological implications, and how their faith can provide both guidance and comfort in dealing with such incidents.

Understanding Sexual Assault: Clearing Myths and Misconceptions

Defining Sexual Assault:

- **Clarity on the Subject**: Sexual assault is any form of sexual activity or contact that occurs without the explicit consent of both parties. It includes a range of behaviors, from unwanted touching to rape.
- **Consent**: It's vital to understand that consent must be freely given, informed, enthusiastic, and continuous. It isn't just the absence of a "no"; it requires an explicit "yes."

Common Myths:

- **Myth**: Provocative clothing or behavior invites assault.
- **Truth**: Nothing justifies or excuses sexual assault. The blame lies solely with the perpetrator.
- **Myth**: Men cannot be victims.
- **Truth**: Men, too, can be, and are, victims of sexual assault. Gender doesn't exempt anyone from being a victim.
- **Myth**: It's not assault if the parties are in a relationship.

- **Truth**: Even within relationships, every act requires consent.

Emotional and Psychological Ramifications

Immediate Effects:

- **Shock and Denial**: Initial reactions can include shock, disbelief, and denial.
- **Guilt and Shame**: Victims might wrongly blame themselves, wondering if they could have done something differently.
- **Anger**: A deep sense of anger, both at the assailant and sometimes inwardly, is common.

Long-Term Effects:

- **Depression**: The trauma can lead to prolonged periods of sadness, hopelessness, and even suicidal thoughts.
- **Anxiety and Panic Attacks**: Constant fear, sometimes culminating in panic attacks, can be a direct result.
- **Relationship Issues**: Trust issues can arise, making it difficult for survivors to form or maintain relationships.

The Church's Role: Offering Support and Sanctuary

Believe the Survivors:

- **Prioritizing Compassion**: Jesus always showed compassion to the hurting and broken. Following His example, the church should prioritize believing and supporting survivors.
- **Avoiding Victim-Blaming**: Remembering that the fault lies solely with the perpetrator ensures a safe space for victims.

Resources and Counseling:

- **Access to Support**: Churches can provide access to Christian counselors trained in trauma and sexual assault.
- **Prayerful Support**: Offering prayers, holding special prayer meetings, or simply being there can make a world of difference.

Teach and Advocate for Respect and Consent

- **Biblical Respect**: The Bible teaches respect for all, with passages like Philippians 2:3, which encourages believers to value others above themselves.
- **Understanding Consent**: Teaching young people about the importance of mutual respect and understanding in relationships is paramount.

Recovery through Faith

The Healing Power of Scripture:

- **Restorative Passages**: Scriptures such as Psalm 34:18 remind us that God is close to the brokenhearted and rescues those crushed in spirit.
- **Fighting Lies with Truth**: When survivors are plagued with self-blame, scriptures can offer truth and perspective.

God's Unchanging Character:

- **Immutable Love**: No matter the trauma, God's love remains unwavering. His love can provide comfort and assurance in the healing process.
- **Jesus, Our Advocate**: 1 John 2:1 reminds us that Jesus is our advocate. He understands pain, betrayal, and suffering, making Him the perfect comforter.

For young individuals navigating the challenges of today's world, understanding the grave realities of sexual assault is of paramount importance. The church, holding the beacon of truth and love, has a vital role in educating, supporting, and healing. Holding tight to biblical principles while approaching this issue with sensitivity ensures that young souls find both wisdom and solace in the face of such adversity.

Edward D. Andrews

SECTION 2 Surviving My Friends

THE OUTSIDER 11 Dealing with Loneliness

Loneliness is a universal human emotion, complex and unique to each individual. For many young people, it can feel all-consuming. In an age where connections seem just a click away, why is it that young souls still grapple with such profound isolation?

Understanding Loneliness

Defining Loneliness:

- Loneliness isn't merely being alone. It's a deep emotional state of feeling disconnected, even when surrounded by people. It's a sense of social or emotional isolation.

The Age of Digital Isolation:

- In an era marked by technological connectivity, true human connection seems to be dwindling. Online interactions can't replace genuine, face-to-face human contact and heartfelt conversations.

Loneliness: A Spiritual Perspective

- It's imperative to realize that feelings of loneliness aren't just psychological or sociological; they can be spiritual too. God created humans for fellowship – with Him and with others.

The Biblical View on Loneliness

- **God Acknowledges Loneliness**: After creating Adam, God declared, "It is not good for man to be alone" (Genesis 2:18). This was the first thing God deemed "not good" after creation, signifying the significance of companionship in human existence.

- **Prominent Biblical Figures Felt Lonely**: Elijah, David, Paul, and even Jesus experienced feelings of isolation. Their stories serve as powerful reminders that loneliness doesn't discriminate.

Factors Contributing to Loneliness in Youth

Societal Pressure and Expectations:

- The pressure to fit in, coupled with an incessant need for validation, amplifies feelings of isolation in those who feel they don't measure up to societal standards.

Transitional Phases:

- Moving to new places, starting at a new school, or navigating the tumultuous waters of adolescence can often lead to feelings of isolation.

Digital World's Illusion:

- Social media platforms portray an illusion of a perfect life, intensifying feelings of being left out among youth.

Facing Loneliness: Conservative Christian Guidance

Seeking God's Presence:

- Remember the promise in Deuteronomy 31:6, "He will never leave you nor forsake you." Seeking God in prayer and Scripture reading can help combat feelings of isolation.

Joining a Church Youth Group:

- Engaging in church activities can foster genuine connections and provide a sense of belonging. It's a space to meet like-minded peers who share similar values.

Limiting Social Media Intake:

- Taking breaks from social media, engaging in digital detoxes, and prioritizing real-life interactions can reduce feelings of isolation and improve mental well-being.

Engage in Service and Outreach:
- Acts of service, whether through the church or community initiatives, can help create connections and combat loneliness. Service is a reflection of Christ's love and can provide purpose and direction.

Professional Counseling Rooted in Faith:
- It's essential to acknowledge when professional help is needed. Christian counseling can provide strategies to cope, rooted in biblical principles.

Fostering Genuine Connections

Building Relationships with Elders:
- Engaging with the elderly in the church or community can offer wisdom, understanding, and a unique bond.

Participating in Group Studies:
- Bible study groups or book clubs can provide regular interaction and deep discussions, promoting genuine friendships.

Seeking Mentoring:
- A mentor can provide guidance, a listening ear, and a deep connection rooted in shared beliefs.

Conclusion

Loneliness can feel like an insurmountable mountain for many young individuals. However, armed with the understanding that God is perpetually with them and the tools provided by the church and Scripture, they can navigate these feelings. By seeking genuine human connections, reducing digital intake, and grounding themselves in their faith, young people can combat the intense feelings of loneliness pervasive in today's society.

Edward D. Andrews

THE OUTSIDER 12 Where Do I Fit In?

The adolescent journey is fraught with the challenges of self-discovery and identity formation. For many young people, the question, "Where do I fit in?" becomes paramount. In a world riddled with expectations, stereotypes, and the continuous bombardment of social media perceptions, finding one's place can seem like an insurmountable task. Let's delve into this intricate issue from a conservative Christian perspective.

The Core of the Question

Understanding the Crux:
- This poignant question isn't merely about social acceptance but taps into deeper aspects of identity, purpose, and spiritual belonging.

The Biblical Perspective:
- God created every individual uniquely, with distinct talents, personalities, and purposes. Psalm 139:14 reminds us, "I am fearfully and wonderfully made." Recognizing this divine hand in our creation aids in understanding our unique place in the world.

Societal Pressures and Their Impact

The Struggle with Conformity:
- In an era where conformity is often mistaken for unity, young people feel pressured to fit predefined molds, often at the cost of suppressing their genuine selves.

Social Media and Virtual Realities:

- Digital platforms often present distorted realities. The constant comparison can amplify feelings of not fitting in, especially when life doesn't mirror the 'perfect' images on screen.

The Dual Struggle of Being a Christian Youth:

- Upholding Christian values in an increasingly secular world can intensify feelings of alienation. However, it's essential to remember Romans 12:2, "Do not conform to the pattern of this world."

God's Design and Individual Purpose

Understanding One's Worth:

- Our worth isn't determined by societal standards but by God's love for us. He has a unique plan for every individual, as Jeremiah 29:11 promises a future and a hope.

God's Kingdom Has Many Members:

- 1 Corinthians 12 speaks of the body of Christ, emphasizing the importance of each member, no matter how seemingly insignificant. Each has a role, and every role is essential.

Practical Steps to Find One's Place

Self-Reflection and Prayer:

- Spending time in prayer and self-reflection can help young individuals understand their strengths, passions, and God's purpose for them.

Engaging in Church Community:

- Churches offer diverse opportunities to serve, learn, and grow. Engaging in these can help in finding one's niche within the broader community.

Seeking Guidance:
- Elders, mentors, or Christian counselors can offer wisdom, guidance, and a fresh perspective in the quest for identity and belonging.

Broadening Horizons:
- Joining Christian youth groups, attending retreats, or participating in mission trips can provide broader perspectives and diverse interactions, helping individuals find their fit.

Coping Mechanisms: Drawing Strength from Scripture

Building a Strong Spiritual Foundation:
- Grounding oneself in Scripture provides a compass. Verses like Romans 8:28, which speaks of all things working together for good, can be particularly comforting.

Developing a Personal Relationship with Jesus:
- Understanding that Jesus, too, was an outsider in many ways, and building a personal relationship with Him can provide solace and understanding.

Remembering Persecuted Christians:
- Reflecting on Christians worldwide who face persecution for their beliefs serves as a sobering reminder and can instill a sense of belonging to a larger, global community of believers.

Conclusion

The journey of self-discovery and finding one's place is multifaceted and challenging. However, it's essential to remember that in God's grand design, every piece fits perfectly. By anchoring oneself in faith, seeking godly counsel, and engaging actively within the Christian community, young individuals can find their unique place in this vast tapestry of life. In this journey, it's crucial to recognize that the eternal question, "Where do I fit in?" finds its most profound answer in the embrace of a loving God.

THE OUTSIDER 13 Why I Struggle with Having Friends

Friendship is a fundamental human need, resonating deeply within our core from the earliest memories of childhood play to more complex relationships in adulthood. Yet, for many young individuals, the quest for genuine friendship becomes an uphill battle, fraught with challenges and punctuated by heartbreak. Let's explore the reasons behind the struggles young Christians face in forming meaningful friendships.

The Essence of Friendship: A Biblical Overview

God's Design for Companionship:

- From the beginning, it's evident that humans were created for relationship. Genesis 2:18 states, "It is not good that the man should be alone." God's design underscores the importance of companionship.

Christ's Model of Friendship:

- Jesus, during His time on earth, modeled what true friendship looks like. He surrounded Himself with disciples, not just as followers but as genuine friends, emphasizing love, loyalty, and sacrifice.

Friendship's Foundational Pillars:

- Proverbs 17:17 tells us, "A friend loves at all times." This foundational element of love, alongside trust, loyalty, and mutual respect, forms the cornerstones of true friendship.

Modern-Day Challenges to Authentic Friendship

The Social Media Mirage:
- The digital age, while offering unprecedented connectivity, often masks the quality of connections. Superficial friendships, governed by 'likes' and 'follows', can leave many feeling isolated amidst a sea of acquaintances.

The Pressure of Conformity:
- Especially during teenage years, the pressure to conform can be immense. Staying true to one's beliefs, especially conservative Christian values, can sometimes result in feelings of alienation.

Fear of Vulnerability:
- Opening up, revealing one's true self, and sharing personal struggles, especially in a judgmental environment, can be daunting. This fear can prevent deep connections.

Navigating Differences:
- In a diverse world, differences in beliefs, values, backgrounds, and perspectives can pose challenges in forming close-knit friendships.

Spiritual Warfare and Friendship:
- The Bible speaks of the spiritual battle that believers face (Ephesians 6:12). Satan, as the adversary, often works to isolate believers, making them feel alone and unsupported.

Navigating the Friendship Labyrinth: Practical Guidance

Seeking Quality over Quantity:
- Instead of pursuing numerous acquaintances, focus on fostering deeper connections with a few. Remember, Jesus had many followers but only a close circle of twelve disciples.

Being Authentic:

- Masking one's true self might result in temporary acceptance but can lead to longer-term feelings of emptiness. It's essential to remain genuine and attract friends who value the real you.

Finding Shared Activities:

- Engaging in church groups, Christian camps, or community service can provide platforms to meet like-minded individuals and form bonds over shared experiences.

Prayer and Guidance:

- Regularly seeking God's guidance through prayer can lead the way to fulfilling friendships. James 1:5 assures us that God gives wisdom generously when we ask.

Building Boundaries:

- While openness is essential, setting boundaries helps in safeguarding oneself from negative influences and toxic relationships.

Engaging in Self-Reflection:

- Periodically taking stock of one's own behavior, attitudes, and expectations in friendships can lead to personal growth and better relational outcomes.

Friendship and the Grand Eternal Perspective

Every struggle faced, including those in friendships, fits into the broader tapestry of God's plan. The trials faced today mold character, resilience, and faith, preparing young believers for the promises of eternity. While navigating friendships, it's crucial to remember the promise in Deuteronomy 31:6, "He will never leave you nor forsake you." God's unwavering friendship remains the gold standard, a beacon of hope in the tumultuous journey of adolescence and young adulthood.

THE OUTSIDER 14 How Many Friends Should I have?

The pursuit of friendship, especially during the turbulent teenage years and early adulthood, often gets intertwined with societal pressures and personal insecurities. One pressing question many youths face is: "How many friends should I have?" This question, though simple on the surface, delves deep into one's self-worth, identity, and purpose.

The Societal Perspective on Friendships

Popularity Contests:

- The modern world, fueled by social media metrics and school hierarchies, sometimes equates self-worth with the number of friends or followers one has. It suggests that more is better.

The Fear of Missing Out (FOMO):

- A rampant issue today is the fear of not being part of a group or missing out on shared experiences, driving many young people to amass a large circle of acquaintances.

Quantity vs. Quality: A Biblical Perspective

Jesus' Circle of Friends:

- Christ, during His ministry, had multitudes that followed Him. Yet, He had a select group of 12 disciples and an even closer circle within them: Peter, James, and John. This shows the difference between general acquaintances and deep, meaningful relationships.

Proverbs on Friendship:

- Proverbs 18:24 states, "A man of many companions may come to ruin, but there is a friend who sticks closer than a brother." This verse underscores the importance of quality over quantity.

The Parable of the Sower:

- The seeds that fell among the thorns in Matthew 13 can be likened to superficial friendships that choke out spiritual growth. Not all friendships bear good fruit.

Navigating Numbers: How Many is Too Many or Too Few?

The Depth of Connection:

- It's not about how many friends one has but the depth of the connection. True friendship thrives on mutual respect, understanding, shared values, and trust.

The Balance of Time:

- Time is a finite resource. Spreading oneself too thin can lead to shallow relationships. Investing time and energy in fewer friends can yield deeper, more meaningful connections.

The Emotional and Spiritual Capacity:

- Everyone has varying capacities to emotionally and spiritually invest in relationships. It's vital to know one's limits and not overburden oneself.

The Importance of Solitude:

- While friendships are crucial, so is solitude. Jesus often withdrew from the crowds to spend time alone in prayer (Luke 5:16). Solitude allows for self-reflection, personal growth, and spiritual deepening.

Practical Tips for Determining Your Friendship Circle

Self-Reflection and Prayer:
- Regular introspection and seeking God's guidance through prayer can provide clarity on the right balance of friendships.

Setting Boundaries:
- Establishing clear boundaries ensures that one is not overwhelmed by the demands of numerous relationships.

Seeking Counsel:
- Talking to mentors, parents, or spiritual leaders can provide a mature perspective on friendships and help in making informed decisions.

Evaluating Fruitfulness:
- Assessing the fruit that each friendship bears, in terms of mutual spiritual growth, support, and encouragement, can guide in determining which relationships to nurture.

The Eternal Perspective on Friendships

In the grand tapestry of life and in the light of eternity, numbers fade into insignificance. What remains eternally significant is the quality of our relationships and their alignment with God's purpose. The Apostle Paul, in his letters, often mentioned specific individuals, indicating deep, personal connections. These weren't mere numbers but relationships forged in the crucible of shared faith and purpose.

In conclusion, the question "How many friends should I have?" doesn't have a one-size-fits-all answer. It varies for each individual based on personal, emotional, and spiritual capacities. What remains paramount is ensuring that each friendship aligns with God's purpose, nurtures mutual growth, and stands the test of time. In the end, it's not about counting friends but making each friendship count.

THE OUTSIDER 15 Others Are Spreading Rumors About Me

Navigating through the tumultuous waters of adolescence and young adulthood is a daunting task in itself. But when compounded with the weight of rumors, it can feel as though one is walking through a storm with no umbrella. Rumors—unsubstantiated stories or claims about someone—can distort perceptions, affect relationships, and erode self-worth.

Understanding the Birth and Spread of Rumors

Why Do People Start Rumors?

- **Insecurity**: Often, people spread rumors as a way to deflect attention from their own insecurities. By discussing others, they hope to elevate their status or divert attention from their shortcomings.
- **Jealousy**: A common driving force behind rumors is envy. If someone possesses qualities or things that another desires, it can lead to the creation of false stories to tarnish their image.
- **A Desire for Control or Power**: Information, even if false, gives the illusion of power. By being a source of "news", individuals feel they wield influence over peers.
- **Boredom**: In some cases, individuals spread rumors simply to introduce excitement or drama into mundane routines.

The Rapid Spread:

- In today's digital age, rumors can spread at lightning speed via social media platforms, making them even more potent and damaging.

The Biblical View on Rumors and Gossip

- **Proverbs 16:28**: "A dishonest man spreads strife, and a whisperer separates close friends." The Bible clearly speaks against those who spread untruths and the division they cause.
- **James 1:26**: "If anyone thinks he is religious and does not bridle his tongue but deceives his heart, this person's religion is worthless." This highlights the importance of guarding one's speech and the potential self-deception in loose talk.

The Emotional and Spiritual Impact of Being the Subject of Rumors

- **Erosion of Self-Worth**: Constant whispers and hushed tones can lead to self-doubt and a plummeting self-esteem.
- **Broken Trust**: Rumors often stem from within one's close circle, leading to shattered trust.
- **Isolation**: The individual becomes an outsider, ostracized based on falsehoods.
- **Spiritual Struggle**: It can also lead to a crisis of faith, where one questions God's justice and presence in their trials.

Navigating the Storm: Coping with Rumors

Seek Truth:

- Before reacting, it's vital to discern the veracity of the rumor. Approaching trusted individuals for clarification can help separate fact from fiction.

Strength in Silence:

- Responding aggressively or defensively can sometimes add fuel to the fire. Proverbs 26:20 notes, "Without wood, a fire goes out; without gossip, a quarrel dies down."

Find Support:
- Surround yourself with true friends and family who can provide emotional and spiritual support.

Confront Calmly:
- If deemed necessary, approach the source of the rumor with calmness and grace, seeking clarity and resolution.

Rise Above:
- Remember that one's worth isn't determined by the words of others but by the truth of God's word and His unconditional love.

Engage in Self-Care:
- Physical activity, prayer, meditation, and engaging in hobbies can act as effective distractions and help in emotional healing.

Seek Counseling:
- A professional can provide tools and strategies to cope with the emotional aftermath of rumors.

A Future Perspective

Remember that rumors, like all trials, are temporal. They will eventually fade. But the lessons learned, the resilience built, and the character developed during such trials will last. Romans 5:3-4 states, "Not only so, but we also glory in our sufferings, because we know that suffering produces perseverance; perseverance, character; and character, hope."

Rumors, though hurtful, can be transformative. When navigated with wisdom, grace, and a reliance on God's truth, they become avenues for profound personal and spiritual growth. The journey from being an outsider to understanding one's worth in God's eyes is a testament to the triumph of truth over deceit.

Edward D. Andrews

THE OUTSIDER 16
Resisting Peer Pressure to Do Wrong

The pull of peer pressure is an age-old challenge, yet its grip remains as potent as ever in the modern world. The urge to belong, to fit in, to be accepted—these are feelings we all grapple with, especially during the formative years of adolescence and early adulthood. The crucible of this pressure often tempts young souls to compromise, to sidestep their values, and to take paths they might later regret.

Understanding Peer Pressure

What is Peer Pressure?

- At its core, peer pressure is the influence exerted by a peer group in encouraging a person to change their attitudes, values, or behaviors in order to conform to group norms.

The Mechanics of Peer Pressure:

- **Direct Pressure**: When someone tells you what behavior is expected, e.g., "Everyone is doing it."
- **Indirect Pressure**: When you're around people who are behaving in a certain way, and you feel the need to fit in.
- **Individual Pressure**: When you pressure yourself into doing something because you fear being left out or ridiculed.

Biblical Perspective on Peer Pressure

- The Bible isn't silent on the topic of peer pressure. Proverbs 1:10 says, "My son, if sinful men entice you, do not give in to them." This scriptural wisdom advises us not to yield to pressures that lead us away from righteousness.

Why is it So Hard to Resist?

- **Desire for Acceptance**: We all want to belong. The fear of ostracization can push one to go against their values.
- **Curiosity**: Sometimes, young minds want to experiment, to see "what's on the other side."
- **Misguided Definitions of Maturity**: Adolescents often mistakenly equate indulging in wrong behaviors with adulthood.

Overcoming the Weight of Peer Pressure

Value Self-Integrity:
- Recognize that your worth isn't determined by external validation but by your integrity and values. Psalm 139:14 reminds us, "I am fearfully and wonderfully made."

Choose Friends Wisely:
- Surround yourself with those who uplift you. Proverbs 13:20 advises, "He who walks with wise men will be wise, but the companion of fools will suffer harm."

Empower Yourself with Knowledge:
- Often, the allure of doing wrong comes from a lack of understanding. Know the consequences, both immediate and long-term, of the actions you're being pressured into.

Seek Wise Counsel:
- Engage in conversations with trusted adults or mentors. Their experiences can offer invaluable insights.

Learn to Say "No":

- It's essential to practice assertiveness. Saying "no" can be empowering and can set the tone for future interactions.

Deepen Your Spiritual Connection:
- Strengthening your relationship with God can act as a buffer against external pressures. Galatians 5:16 advises, "So I say, walk by the Spirit, and you will not gratify the desires of the flesh."

Practical Tools to Resist Peer Pressure:
- **Visualization**: Before attending an event or going out, visualize possible scenarios and rehearse your responses.
- **Buddy System**: Go out with friends who share your values. There's strength in numbers.
- **Exit Strategy**: Always have a way out. This could be a text code with a parent or friend to get you out of uncomfortable situations.
- **Delay**: If pressed to make a decision, it's okay to ask for time.

Reaffirming Personal Values

Reconnect with your values. Take time to introspect, to write down what you stand for, and the type of person you want to become. This personal charter can serve as a compass during tumultuous times.

Seeking Healing if You've Succumbed

We're all fallible. If you've given in to peer pressure, it's vital to know that God's love and grace are boundless. 1 John 1:9 assures, "If we confess our sins, he is faithful and just to forgive us our sins and to cleanse us from all unrighteousness."

In a world replete with pressures, standing firm in one's values might seem an uphill task. Yet, with the right tools, a deep connection to one's values, and an unwavering faith in God, the weight of peer pressure can be countered. As Romans 12:2 reminds us, "Do not be conformed to this world, but be transformed by the renewal of your mind."

SECTION 3 Surviving the Family

Edward D. Andrews

THE OUTSIDER 17 Viewing the House Rules in a New Light

THE OUTSIDER 18 Getting Along with My Brothers and Sisters

Navigating the transition between childhood and adulthood can be likened to walking a tightrope. One of the common sources of contention in this delicate balance is grappling with the house rules set by parents or guardians. For many young people, these rules can feel stifling, arbitrary, or even oppressive. Yet, viewing these guidelines in a new light can be transformative, leading to growth, understanding, and a harmonious living environment.

The Nature and Purpose of House Rules

Why Do Parents Set Rules?

- **Safety**: Above all, parents desire to keep their children safe. Rules are often set to prevent harm, both physical and emotional.
- **Character Building**: Rules can cultivate discipline, responsibility, and other virtues, preparing young people for the larger world.
- **Maintaining Order**: With multiple personalities under one roof, rules ensure a harmonious living environment.
- **Spiritual Growth**: For Christian households, some rules are rooted in faith, aimed at guiding young people in their spiritual journey.

Misunderstandings Surrounding House Rules

Often, the tension arises not from the rule itself but from misunderstandings about its purpose.

- **Perceiving Rules as Arbitrary**: Young people might see rules as whimsical decisions of parents rather than carefully thought-out guidelines.
- **Equating Freedom with Absence of Rules**: There's a misconception that true freedom means no restrictions. Yet, freedom thrives within boundaries.
- **The "Other Parents" Comparison**: "But Jake's parents let him do it!" Such comparisons can make one's own household rules seem overly strict.

Benefits of House Rules

A Structured Environment:
- Just as traffic rules prevent chaos on the road, house rules prevent chaos at home.

A Safe Space:
- Rules around visitors, outings, or online interactions are often designed to protect young people from potential dangers.

Preparation for the Real World:
- The world is full of rules. Navigating house rules prepares one for larger societal norms and regulations.

Fostering Mutual Respect:
- When everyone adheres to a set of guidelines, it fosters an environment of mutual respect.

Reframing Our Perspective on House Rules

Seeking Understanding:
- Instead of rebelling, seek to understand the rationale behind a rule. Open dialogue can shed light on its purpose.

Acknowledging the Temporary Nature:
- Most house rules are for a season. As you grow and demonstrate responsibility, many rules might evolve or even be lifted.

Finding Balance:
- It's essential to strike a balance between adhering to rules and expressing one's individuality. This doesn't mean breaking rules but negotiating adjustments as one matures.

Embracing the Spiritual Aspect:
- For Christian young people, adhering to house rules can be seen as honoring one's parents, aligning with the fifth commandment in Exodus 20:12, "Honor your father and your mother."

Engaging in Constructive Dialogue

Approaching with Respect:
- When discussing a particular rule, approach parents with respect, acknowledging their position while expressing your perspective.

Seeking Compromise:
- Is there a middle ground? Can the rule be adjusted as you demonstrate responsibility?

Emphasizing Personal Growth:

- Showcase your maturity. If you feel a rule is outdated due to your growth, present your case. However, be open to feedback.

Scriptural Insights on Obedience and Respect

The Bible offers wisdom on the dynamics between children and parents. Ephesians 6:1-3 advises, "Children, obey your parents in the Lord, for this is right. 'Honor your father and mother' — which is the first commandment with a promise — 'so that it may go well with you and that you may enjoy long life on the earth.'"

Conclusion

House rules, though sometimes challenging for young people to grapple with, are tools of love, guidance, and protection. By viewing them in a new light, understanding their purpose, and engaging in open dialogue, young people can navigate these boundaries with grace, maturity, and wisdom. Remember, these rules are often the scaffolding, ensuring you grow straight and strong, ready to face the world beyond the safety of home.

THE OUTSIDER 19 How Do I Find Privacy?

As young people transition from childhood to adolescence and onward to young adulthood, the quest for personal privacy grows. The journey from dependency to autonomy is a natural part of maturation, and privacy plays a significant role in this progression. Within the bounds of safety and propriety, seeking and respecting privacy is essential for fostering individuality, responsibility, and trust.

Understanding the Need for Privacy

Why Privacy Matters:

1. **Personal Growth:** A private space or time allows young individuals to introspect, reflect on their beliefs, and cultivate their identity without constant external influence.
2. **Emotional Health:** Moments of solitude can offer a respite from external pressures, reducing stress and promoting mental well-being.
3. **Building Trust:** When parents and guardians allow young individuals certain privacies, it signifies trust, fostering a healthier relationship.

The Biblical Perspective:

While Scripture does not explicitly discuss personal privacy as we understand it today, it does hint at the importance of solitude and introspection. Jesus, for instance, often retreated to solitary places to pray and reflect (Luke 5:16).

Challenges to Privacy

Living in a Digital Age:

With the rise of social media and constant connectivity, maintaining privacy can be a challenge. Everything, from personal feelings to daily activities, can be broadcasted in seconds.

Family Dynamics:

In larger families or smaller homes, physical space can be limited. This can make it challenging to find moments or areas of seclusion.

Overprotective Parents:

Out of love and concern, some parents may unintentionally invade their child's privacy, be it through constant questioning, room checks, or monitoring online activities.

Navigating Privacy Concerns

Open Communication:

Discuss your needs with family members. Be honest about why you're seeking privacy and listen to their concerns as well. Understanding often comes from mutual respect and dialogue.

Setting Boundaries:

Both in the physical and digital realm, it's essential to set and respect boundaries. This includes not sharing every detail of one's life online and having spaces at home where you can be alone.

Respecting Others' Privacy:

Just as you seek privacy, ensure you respect the privacy of others, be it siblings, parents, or friends.

Safety First:

While seeking privacy, especially online, always prioritize safety. Be cautious about sharing personal information, and be aware of who has access to your data.

Biblical Wisdom on Privacy and Secrecy:

It's crucial to distinguish between the pursuit of privacy and the temptation of secrecy. Proverbs 10:9 says, "Whoever walks in integrity walks securely, but whoever takes crooked paths will be found out." While it's natural to want privacy, one should avoid activities that, if brought into the light, would be a cause for shame or regret.

Striking a Balance:

Privacy is not about isolation but about finding a balance. While it's okay to seek moments of solitude, ensure it doesn't lead to prolonged isolation, which can be detrimental.

Fostering Trust with Parents:

1. **Open up Occasionally**: Letting parents into your life from time to time can alleviate some of their concerns.
2. **Show Responsibility**: Demonstrating maturity can reassure parents, making them more inclined to grant you more privacy.
3. **Seek Mutual Respect**: Understand that just as you have concerns and needs, so do your parents. A mutual understanding can lead to a harmonious balance.

Finding Privacy in Christ:

For Christian young people, one of the most profound forms of privacy can be found in a personal relationship with Christ. In Matthew 6:6, Jesus says, "But when you pray, go into your room, close the door and pray to your Father, who is unseen." This underscores the significance of a personal, private connection with God.

In the challenging journey of coming-of-age, the quest for privacy plays an instrumental role. While the surroundings and circumstances may sometimes seem stifling, with mutual respect, understanding, and trust, young individuals can find their private space. This space, both physical and metaphorical, can be a sanctuary for growth, reflection, and deepening one's relationship with God. The key is to seek privacy not for the sake of rebellion or secrecy but as a tool for personal and spiritual growth.

THE OUTSIDER 20 My Parents Will Not Allow Me to Do Anything

Growing up often feels like a series of doors waiting to be opened. For young individuals, particularly those between the ages of 12 and 25, the journey of self-discovery is intrinsically linked with the urge to experience new things. Yet, for many, the journey often comes with the realization: "My parents won't let me do anything!" Understanding this sentiment, and navigating it from a conservative Christian perspective, requires a balanced exploration of both parental and youthful perspectives.

Understanding the Protective Parental Stance

Rooted in Love:

Parents often set boundaries out of genuine concern and love for their children. They've likely seen more of the world, and its potential dangers, than their children have.

Biblical Mandate:

Scripture instructs parents to "train up a child in the way he should go" (Proverbs 22:6). This means guiding them in the paths of righteousness, and sometimes that involves setting limits.

Fear of the Unknown:

In today's rapidly evolving culture, many things are unfamiliar to parents, leading them to establish rules based on what they know and understand.

The Past as a Mirror:

Parents might reflect on their own youth, the mistakes they made, or the dangers they witnessed, and this can influence the boundaries they set.

The Youth's Perspective

Quest for Independence:

As young individuals mature, a natural inclination is to desire more autonomy and freedom. This is a God-given drive that aids in the process of becoming responsible adults.

Feeling Misunderstood:

The sentiment, "They don't understand me," is common among young people, especially when they feel their ambitions and desires are curtailed by parental restrictions.

Peer Pressure:

The need to fit in and not feel left out is substantial at this age. When peers are allowed to do certain things, the feeling of being restricted becomes even more pronounced.

Seeking Experience:

Youth often feel that they need to experience things firsthand to understand them truly, leading to frustration when these experiences are limited.

Navigating the Restrictions

Open Dialogue:

Encouraging an open channel of communication between parents and children is vital. Both parties should be given a safe space to express their feelings and concerns.

Seek Understanding:

Rather than merely feeling frustrated, young people can seek to understand the reasons behind their parents' restrictions. Asking questions and genuinely listening can lead to a deeper appreciation of their parents' concerns.

Demonstrate Maturity:

Actions often speak louder than words. By showing responsibility and maturity in smaller matters, young people might find their parents more open to granting freedoms in more significant areas.

Seek Godly Counsel:

There's value in seeking wisdom from mature believers or church leaders. They can offer a balanced perspective and might even act as mediators in discussions with parents.

Biblical Examples and Principles

Jesus' Submission:

Even Jesus, the Son of God, was subject to His earthly parents. Luke 2:51 says, "Then He went down with them and came to Nazareth, and was subject to them." This highlights the importance of respecting parental authority, even when it feels limiting.

Wisdom Over Freedom:

Proverbs is a treasure trove of advice on heeding instruction. Proverbs 1:8-9 says, "My son, hear the instruction of your father, And do not forsake the law of your mother; For they will be a graceful ornament on your head, And chains about your neck." Often, parental restrictions are the chains that protect rather than bind.

Consider the Long-Term:

Ecclesiastes 3:1 reminds us, "To everything there is a season, A time for every purpose under heaven." There will be a season for greater freedom, but perhaps now is the season for learning, growing, and understanding.

While the feelings of restrictions can be stifling for young people, it's essential to remember that most parental boundaries are set out of love and concern. By fostering open communication, seeking understanding, and grounding oneself in biblical principles, young individuals can navigate these feelings constructively. Both parents and their children are on a journey, growing and learning together. With mutual respect, understanding, and a shared foundation in Christ, the path can lead to a place of trust, freedom, and deeper love.

Edward D. Andrews

THE OUTSIDER 21 How Can I Cope with Heartbreak?

Heartbreak is an unfortunate rite of passage in the journey of life, especially during the formative years of adolescence and young adulthood. Whether it stems from the end of a romantic relationship, a fallout with a dear friend, or any other deep personal loss, the pain can be overwhelming and at times, unbearable. For many young believers, reconciling this pain with their faith can be challenging. This chapter aims to provide solace and guidance to those navigating the treacherous waters of heartbreak.

Understanding the Nature of Heartbreak

The Emotional Rollercoaster:

Heartbreak is more than just sadness; it's a mix of numerous emotions, including grief, anger, confusion, and even periods of denial. It's essential to recognize and acknowledge these feelings instead of suppressing them.

A Universal Experience:

Everyone, at some point or another, faces heartbreak. It's an intrinsic part of the human experience and transcends age, gender, culture, and socioeconomic status.

A Catalyst for Growth:

While intensely painful, heartbreak can also be a significant source of personal growth and self-reflection. It's a juncture where many re-evaluate what they truly value and desire in relationships and life.

The Spiritual Perspective of Heartbreak

God's Understanding:

Scripture assures us that God is well-acquainted with our sorrows. Psalm 34:18 declares, "The Lord is near to the brokenhearted and saves the crushed in spirit." This is a profound reminder that in our most profound pain, we are not alone.

The Example of Jesus:

Christ Himself experienced deep emotional pain. The Bible describes Jesus as "a man of sorrows, acquainted with grief" (Isaiah 53:3). When Lazarus died, even knowing He would raise him, Jesus wept (John 11:35).

Purpose in Pain:

Romans 8:28 assures us, "And we know that in all things God works for the good of those who love him." Even in heartbreak, God can work for our good, molding our character and drawing us closer to Him.

Practical Steps to Cope with Heartbreak

Seek Support:

Engage with a supportive community, whether that be close friends, family, or church members. Sharing your pain with others can lighten the burden.

Dive into Scripture:

The Bible is filled with comforting verses and stories of individuals who faced and overcame heart-wrenching pain. David's psalms can be especially relatable during such times.

Prayer and Reflection:

Use this time to grow closer to God. Lay your pain before Him, and seek His comfort and guidance.

Maintain Routine:

While the temptation might be to withdraw from daily activities, maintaining a routine can provide a necessary structure and a sense of normalcy.

Avoid Rash Decisions:

Heartbreak can cloud judgment. Avoid making any hasty decisions that you might later regret.

Seek Professional Counseling:

If the pain becomes too overwhelming or persistent, consider seeking professional counseling. A counselor can provide coping strategies and a safe space to process your emotions.

Reframing Heartbreak

A Chance to Realign with God's Will:

Sometimes relationships or situations break down because they aren't in line with God's plan for our lives. Heartbreak can be a process through which God redirects us to His perfect will.

Building Resilience:

Every challenge faced and overcome strengthens our character. Resilience isn't built during times of ease, but in the crucible of adversity.

Preparation for the Future:

The lessons learned from heartbreak can prepare us for future relationships, equipping us with a deeper understanding of ourselves and a clearer idea of what we seek in relationships.

While heartbreak is undeniably painful, it doesn't have to be debilitating. Through faith, support, and a proactive approach to healing, young individuals can not only recover from heartbreak but emerge from it stronger, wiser, and more aligned with God's purpose for their lives. As Psalm 147:3 beautifully articulates, "He heals the brokenhearted and binds up their wounds." With God by our side, recovery and healing are not just possibilities; they are promises.

THE OUTSIDER 22 Coping with My Parent's Divorce

Divorce, while common in today's society, remains a profound and life-altering experience, especially for children and young adults. When two people who were once in love decide to part ways, the emotional, spiritual, and psychological impact can be immense on their offspring. For a young Christian, this can be a particularly challenging test of faith and understanding.

Understanding the Divorce Experience

The World Shattered:

For many young people, their parents' marriage serves as a foundational bedrock — a constant in a world of variables. When this foundation crumbles, it's not uncommon to feel as if the entire world is falling apart.

A Myriad of Emotions:

Sadness, anger, confusion, guilt, and even relief are among the myriad of emotions one might experience. Each feeling is valid, and it's crucial to recognize and process them.

The Desire for Normalcy:

A significant challenge for teens and young adults is the yearning for things to go back to "normal." Adjusting to a new norm can be a daunting task.

Spiritual Implications and Questions

God's Design for Marriage:

The Bible clearly delineates marriage as a lifelong bond. Malachi 2:16 states that God hates divorce. It's important to clarify that while God dislikes the act due to the pain it causes, He remains compassionate towards those affected by it.

The Question of "Why?":

"Why did God allow this?" This is a question many young believers grapple with. While we might not always understand His plans, we can trust in His love and wisdom.

Prayer and Guidance:

Using this challenging time to lean into prayer can be therapeutic. Philippians 4:6-7 reminds us to present our requests to God, and His peace will guard our hearts.

Navigating the Practical and Emotional Challenges

Acceptance and Grief:

Grieving the end of your parents' marriage is natural. This process can be likened to mourning the death of a loved one. Allow yourself the time and space to grieve.

Staying Neutral:

It's essential to remember that the divorce is a decision between your parents. As difficult as it may be, try to avoid taking sides.

Seeking Support:

There's no shame in seeking support. Surrounding oneself with understanding friends, joining support groups, or engaging in counseling can provide relief.

Maintaining Boundaries:

During the turmoil of a divorce, some parents might overshare or lean too heavily on their children for emotional support. It's essential to set healthy boundaries during this time.

Embracing God's Unwavering Love

God's Constant Presence:

In the midst of change and uncertainty, one thing remains unwavering: God's love for you. Deuteronomy 31:8 assures us that God will never leave nor forsake us.

Seeking Solace in Scripture:

Verses like Psalm 34:18 ("The Lord is close to the brokenhearted") can offer immense comfort. Spending time in God's word can be a source of strength.

Connecting with a Spiritual Community:

Now, more than ever, staying connected with a faith community can provide much-needed support and understanding.

Looking Forward

Hope for the Future:

While the present might seem bleak, it's vital to hold onto hope for a brighter future. God can bring beauty out of ashes (Isaiah 61:3).

Learning and Growth:

This experience, as painful as it is, can also be a period of immense personal growth. Resilience, understanding, empathy, and maturity are often forged in the crucible of adversity.

Coping with a parent's divorce is undoubtedly one of the most challenging experiences a young person can face. However, with faith, support, and time, healing is not just a possibility but a promise. The journey might be long and fraught with challenges, but with God as the guide, there's always hope for a brighter tomorrow

Edward D. Andrews

THE OUTSIDER 23 What If My Father or Mother Is Terminally Ill?

Facing the prospect of a terminally ill parent is one of the most heart-wrenching experiences anyone, especially a young person, can undergo. It challenges the core of our beliefs, our sense of stability, and our understanding of life's impermanence. But even in the midst of such anguish, there is hope, comfort, and strength to be found in our faith and the support of those around us.

Understanding Terminal Illness

Defining the Term:

A terminal illness is a disease or condition that cannot be cured or adequately treated and that is reasonably expected to result in the death of the patient. This can range from certain cancers to advanced stages of diseases like Alzheimer's.

The Emotional Roller Coaster:

Upon hearing such news, emotions can range from disbelief to anger, from sadness to hope for a miracle. These feelings aren't linear; they can oscillate from one to another within a matter of moments.

Spiritual Implications and Questions

Questioning God's Plan:

"Why would God allow this?" It's a question that many grapple with. While we may not fully understand His plan, it's important to remember Romans 8:28, which says that in all things, God works for the good of those who love Him.

The Promised Resurrection:

The Bible promises a resurrection for those who have passed away. John 5:28-29 speaks of a time when all in their graves will hear Jesus' voice and come out.

Seeking Comfort in Prayer:

During these challenging times, prayer becomes even more crucial. It's a way to communicate our deepest fears, hopes, and feelings to our Heavenly Father.

Navigating the Emotional and Practical Challenges

Dealing with Grief Before the Loss:

Anticipatory grief is the deep sadness and mourning one feels before the actual loss. This can be as profound and complicated as the grief experienced after the loss.

The Importance of Communication:

As challenging as it may be, it's crucial to discuss feelings, plans, and fears both with the ill parent and other family members.

Finding Support:

Support groups, close friends, church communities, and professional counseling can provide invaluable assistance and understanding during this time.

Making the Most of the Time Left:

Cherishing and making the most of the moments left can create lasting memories. This might include conversations, shared experiences, or even simple acts of love and kindness.

Embracing God's Promises and Compassion

God's Compassionate Nature:

In times of distress, remember Psalm 34:18 – "The Lord is close to the brokenhearted and saves those who are crushed in spirit."

The Hope of Eternity:

While the pain of the present is palpable, focusing on the eternal promises of God can bring solace. 1 Corinthians 2:9 says, "No eye has seen, no ear has heard, and no mind has imagined what God has prepared for those who love him."

Jesus' Example of Grief:

Even Jesus, when faced with the death of his friend Lazarus, wept (John 11:35). This shows that grief is a natural, human response, and even our Savior experienced it.

Looking Forward

Life After the Loss:

The eventual loss of a parent is a profound pain. Yet, with time, the acute pain of grief can give way to a more muted, manageable sorrow interspersed with memories of joy and love.

Building Resilience:

While nothing can take away the pain of such a loss, it can serve as a point of growth, fostering resilience, empathy, and a deeper appreciation for life and love.

Leaning on Faith:

When all seems lost, leaning into faith can provide the strength needed to persevere. Psalm 147:3 reminds us, "He heals the brokenhearted and binds up their wounds."

THE OUTSIDER

The journey through a parent's terminal illness is fraught with heartache, challenges, and a myriad of emotions. Yet, even in the shadow of such pain, God's love, promises, and the support of a caring community can guide, comfort, and strengthen the hurting heart. Remember always that you are not alone; God is ever-present, and His love is unfailing.

őEdward D. Andrews

SECTION 4 Surviving School

THE OUTSIDER 24 How Do I Deal with Bullies?

Facing Bullies: James' Story

One morning, Tom threatened James, saying, "If you come to school tomorrow, I'll hurt you bad." The next day, despite immense fear that made him physically sick, James went to school. Such traumatic events, varying in intensity, occur daily. Over 3.2 million students face bullying each year. Shockingly, around 160,000 teens skip school daily due to bullying. In the digital age, cyberbullying is on the rise, with 52% of young people reporting such incidents.

Defining Bullying

Bullying isn't just about physical harm. It's an unwanted, aggressive behavior among kids, usually showing a power imbalance. It either recurs or has the potential to. The victim and the bully both can face long-term issues. Key elements defining bullying are:

- **Power Imbalance**: Bullies exploit their power to intimidate others. This power could be physical strength, knowledge of someone's secrets, or popularity.
- **Repetition**: It's either a recurring behavior or possesses the potential to recur.
- **Types of Actions**: Bullying can range from threats, rumors, verbal or physical attacks, to deliberate exclusion from a group.

Different Bullying Types

1. **Physical Bullies**: These bullies resort to violent behaviors like:
    - Hitting, kicking, pinching

- Spitting, pushing, tripping
- Damaging someone's belongings
- Making rude gestures

2. **Verbal Bullies**: They employ negative words to dominate:
   - Teasing and name-calling
   - Making inappropriate remarks
   - Threatening harm

3. **Relationship Bullies**: They manipulate relationships to maintain dominance:
   - Spreading rumors
   - Aiming to embarrass and shame others

4. **Reactive Victims**: Some, after facing bullying, turn into bullies themselves. This isn't a justification, merely an observation.

5. **Cyberbullying**: Using technology to harass:
   - Sending mean emails or texts
   - Posting hurtful content on social platforms
   - Spreading online rumors
   - Sharing non-consensual photos

6. **Social Isolation**: Excluding someone to hurt them:
   - Purposeful exclusion from activities or groups
   - Encouraging others to avoid someone
   - Spreading rumors
   - Publicly embarrassing someone

The Global Reach of Bullying

Bullying is not restricted to one region; it's a global issue. Boys, on average, face 11% bullying rates, with Austria reporting the highest at 21%. Girls generally report lower bullying rates. Addressing and understanding this problem is crucial to creating safer environments for children worldwide.

Understanding Bullying and How to Counteract It

Reasons Why People Bully

1. **Past Experience**: Some bully because they were victims at one point, thinking it might offer them a safety net in social situations.

2. **Poor Role Models**: If a child observes bullying at home, either between siblings or from parents, they might emulate that behavior.

3. **Insecurities**: Often, bullies seek to mask their feelings of inadequacy by dominating others.

4. **Desire for Power**: Some individuals bully because they crave control and power, targeting those who appear weaker.

5. **Seeking Popularity**: To fit in with a certain group or gain popularity, some resort to bullying as a misguided way to impress peers.

6. **Thrill-Seeking**: Some privileged individuals resort to bullying for a sense of excitement or to alleviate boredom.

7. **Targeting Differences**: Differences, whether in terms of height, race, religion, beliefs, or background, can unfortunately make someone a target for bullying.

Responding to Bullying

Understanding that bullying is temporary and often fades after high school can be a solace. If possible, ignoring a bully can be effective, as they often seek reactions. It's essential to discern between empty threats and genuine threats. Here are some pointers:

- **Non-Reaction**: If a bully doesn't get the reaction they desire, they may lose interest.
- **Avoid Revenge**: Seeking revenge might escalate the situation, making it harder to resolve.
- **Safe Paths**: Adjust your routes to avoid places where known bullies congregate.
- **Stay Calm**: Avoid making antagonistic comments that could incite the bully.
- **Be Observant**: If you witness bullying, even if you're not the victim, consider reporting it. Recording evidence discreetly can be valuable.

Self-Defense and Building Resilience

While it's vital to try non-confrontational methods first, there may be times when standing up becomes necessary. Building physical strength and staying fit can deter potential bullies. Also, learning self-defense techniques can be empowering. While the world might have changed from simpler times, having the tools to defend oneself is invaluable.

Many correctional officers, for instance, undergo Aikido training – a Japanese martial art – to handle aggressive inmates. Similarly, equipping children with self-defense skills can prepare them for unforeseen challenges. In an unpredictable world, it's always better to be prepared than caught off guard.

Empower Your Children Against Bullying

Proactive Parenting Measures

As parents, it's crucial to equip your child with the skills to handle bullies from an early age. It's unwise to assume, "It's not my child's concern." One impactful way is to ensure your child maintains a healthy diet and follows a regular exercise regime. Notably, bullies are less inclined to target children who are physically fit. Simple actions like instructing your child to maintain a good posture, make eye contact, and communicate assertively can alter the way they are perceived by their peers. It's essential to provide them with a realistic understanding of the world, rather than an idealized perspective. Preparing them for real-world scenarios is not just beneficial but a necessary act of love.

Training for Self-Assurance

Right upbringing can empower your child not only to face bullies but also to shield others from such adversities. For parents who want to ensure their child is always a step ahead, enrolling them in unarmed self-defense classes can be invaluable. Even a couple of years of wrestling during grade school can equip a child to hold their own against larger opponents. Integrating disciplines like Aikido, wrestling, and basic boxing can enhance your child's physical fitness and, if ever required, could be life-saving.

Edward D. Andrews

THE OUTSIDER 25 How Can I Cope with School When I Hate It?

School, an institution designed for learning and growth, often becomes a battleground for many young people. The struggles can range from academic pressures to social challenges. But amidst these challenges, there's a silver lining, a hope that can guide us through the toughest of times.

Understanding the Struggles

The Weight of Academic Pressure:

Many students feel buried under the weight of homework, tests, and the never-ending demand for excellence. This pressure is further intensified by the expectation to excel in every subject.

Social Anxieties and Peer Dynamics:

From trying to fit in, to dealing with bullies or the challenges of making true friends, school can often feel like a maze of intricate social dynamics.

Lack of Interest:

Not every subject resonates with every student. The challenge of finding relevance and interest in subjects that don't align with one's passions can be daunting.

Physical and Emotional Health:

Issues like sleep deprivation, stress, and even more severe mental health issues can severely affect a student's experience at school.

Facing Challenges Head-On

Building a Routine:

Establishing a routine can help in bringing order to chaos. Allocating specific times for study, breaks, and leisure can make the day more predictable and manageable.

Seeking Help:

There's no shame in admitting when you need help. This could be academic help, like tutoring, or emotional support from counselors, teachers, or trusted individuals.

Focusing on Strengths:

While it's essential to work on areas of weakness, it's equally important to focus on strengths. Celebrate subjects or activities where you excel.

Creating a Support System:

Friends, family, and faith communities can be anchors in turbulent times. Sharing concerns, seeking advice, or even just having someone to talk to can be invaluable.

Spiritual Solutions and Insights

Prayer and Meditation:

Prayer isn't just about asking for help; it's about seeking guidance, finding peace, and reconnecting with our purpose. Philippians 4:6-7 reminds us to present our requests to God, promising the peace of God in return.

Biblical Examples of Overcoming Adversity:

Look to figures like Joseph, who faced immense challenges but rose above them due to his unwavering faith and integrity.

Finding Purpose:

Sometimes, understanding the bigger picture helps in navigating smaller challenges. Recognize that school is just a phase, a preparation ground for the future God has in store.

Practical Ways to Enhance the School Experience

Engage in Extracurriculars:

Activities outside of the regular curriculum, be it sports, arts, or clubs, can provide an outlet for passion and create a more balanced school experience.

Setting Realistic Goals:

Instead of aiming for perfection in every area, set achievable goals. Celebrate small victories.

Communicate with Teachers:

If a particular subject or area is challenging, communicate with your teacher. They might offer insights, resources, or even just understanding that can make a difference.

Seeking Solace in Scriptures:

Verses like Jeremiah 29:11, which speaks of God's plans to prosper and not harm, to give hope and a future, can be a beacon of hope in challenging times.

Finding the Silver Lining

Life Skills and Preparation:

School isn't just about academics; it's a training ground for life. From time management to interpersonal skills, the challenges faced now prepare for future hurdles.

Building Character:

Romans 5:3-4 speaks of suffering producing perseverance, character, and hope. The trials faced in school can be foundational in character building.

Conclusion

The struggles with school are real, but they aren't insurmountable. With a mix of practical strategies, spiritual insights, and a supportive community, even the most challenging school days can be navigated with grace and resilience. Remember always that this season, like all others, shall pass, and what remains are the lessons learned and the character built.

THE OUTSIDER 26 I Am Thinking of Quitting School

The thought of quitting school is not an unfamiliar one to many young people. At some point, whether because of academic pressures, social challenges, or personal circumstances, the idea surfaces. And while it's essential to empathize with these feelings, it's also crucial to approach such a significant decision with clarity, wisdom, and guidance.

The Roots of the Desire to Quit

Overwhelming Academic Pressure:

The relentless chase for grades, excellence, and achievement can make school feel less like a place of learning and more like an unending race.

Bullying and Social Struggles:

Feeling isolated, bullied, or marginalized can make school seem unbearable. The pain of being an 'outsider' can overshadow the purpose of education.

Personal and Home Challenges:

Difficulties at home, such as family struggles, financial issues, or health challenges, can make the additional stress of school feel insurmountable.

Lack of Interest or Vision:

Some students struggle to see the relevance of what they're learning, making the effort feel meaningless.

Addressing the Feelings Head-On

Seeking Counsel and Wisdom:

Proverbs 11:14 says, "Where there is no guidance, a people falls, but in an abundance of counselors there is safety." It's essential to talk to trusted adults, mentors, or counselors about the feelings of wanting to quit.

Re-evaluating Personal Strengths and Interests:

God has endowed each individual with unique gifts and talents. Sometimes, considering alternative education paths that align better with one's passions might be worth exploring.

Considering the Long-Term Implications:

While the current pain and struggle are real, it's crucial to weigh these against the long-term repercussions of quitting school.

God's Perspective on Perseverance and Wisdom

The Bible holds numerous examples of individuals who faced seemingly insurmountable challenges but found strength in their faith and relationship with God.

Joseph: Despite being sold into slavery and unjustly imprisoned, Joseph's perseverance led him to a position of influence, which he used to save nations.

Paul: In his missionary journeys, Paul faced countless hardships. Yet, his dedication to spreading the Gospel was unwavering.

Scripture also values wisdom and understanding. Proverbs 4:7 states, "Wisdom is the principal thing; therefore get wisdom. And in all your getting, get understanding." School is one avenue to gain knowledge and understanding.

Practical Steps to Rediscover Purpose in School

Setting Short-Term Goals:

Instead of viewing school as a long, drawn-out process, breaking it down into manageable goals can help in finding immediate purpose and motivation.

Seeking Academic Support:

There's no shame in seeking help. Tutoring, extra classes, or even discussing challenges with teachers can make a significant difference.

Engaging in Extracurricular Activities:

Joining clubs, sports, or other activities can provide a break from academic pressures and offer a sense of belonging.

Prioritizing Mental and Emotional Well-being:

Taking care of one's mental and emotional health is paramount. This could mean seeking professional counseling, engaging in hobbies, or spending time in prayer and meditation.

Rekindling Faith Amidst School Challenges:

God's unchanging character can be a source of comfort. Meditating on scriptures, engaging in youth groups, or just spending quiet time in prayer can rejuvenate the spirit.

The feelings of wanting to quit school are genuine and valid. Yet, the decision to do so has long-term implications. With prayer, guidance, and a proactive approach to addressing challenges, it's possible to navigate these feelings and find renewed purpose in education. Remember, God's plans for each individual are for welfare and not for evil, to give a future and a hope (Jeremiah 29:11). Let this promise be a guiding light in times of uncertainty.

THE OUTSIDER 27 How Can I Improve My Grades?

Achieving good grades is often seen as a measure of one's academic prowess and, by extension, one's potential for future success. But what happens when those grades don't reflect your true abilities or aspirations? The journey to improving grades isn't just about working harder; it's about working smarter and seeking God's wisdom and direction in all endeavors.

Understanding the Importance of Good Grades

Before diving into strategies for improvement, it's essential to understand why good grades matter.

A Reflection of Commitment:

Good grades can showcase your dedication, hard work, and commitment to excellence. The Bible says, "Whatever you do, work heartily, as for the Lord and not for men" (Colossians 3:23). This principle applies to our academic pursuits as well.

Opening Opportunities:

Higher grades can lead to more opportunities, such as scholarships, college admissions, and even specific job prospects in the future.

Building a Strong Foundation:

A solid academic foundation can set the stage for lifelong learning and critical thinking skills vital in all areas of life.

Strategies for Improving Grades

Developing Effective Study Habits:

Schedule Regular Study Times: Consistency is key. Establishing regular study times can make studying a habit rather than a chore.

Designate a Study Space: Find a quiet, well-lit area free from distractions.

Use Study Aids: Tools like flashcards, study apps, and mnemonic devices can boost memory retention.

Active Participation in Classes:

Engaging in class discussions, asking questions, and taking diligent notes can significantly enhance understanding and retention of information.

Stay Organized:

Prioritize Tasks: Use planners or digital tools to keep track of assignments, test dates, and other essential academic activities.

Break Tasks into Manageable Chunks: Instead of cramming the night before an exam, break your study sessions into smaller, more focused sessions.

Seek Help When Needed:

There's no shame in seeking help. Form study groups, attend review sessions, or consider hiring a tutor if possible.

Maintaining a Healthy Lifestyle:

Quality sleep, a balanced diet, and regular exercise can significantly impact academic performance. The body, mind, and spirit are interconnected, and taking care of one often benefits the others.

Stay Spiritually Connected:

Include God in your academic journey. Regular prayer and meditation can provide clarity, reduce anxiety, and guide decision-making.

Prayerful Consideration and Trusting in God

Psalm 121:2 reminds us, "My help comes from the Lord, the Maker of heaven and earth." In our academic pursuits, as in all things, it's crucial to lean on God and seek His guidance.

A Reflective Approach to Mistakes:

Mistakes and setbacks are a part of life. Instead of seeing them as failures, view them as opportunities to learn, grow, and lean further into God's grace.

Setting Realistic Expectations:

While striving for excellence is commendable, it's also essential to set achievable goals. Celebrate small victories along the way and remember that your worth isn't determined by grades alone but by God's unending love for you.

God's Perspective on Wisdom and Diligence:

The Scriptures are filled with verses that extol the virtues of wisdom, understanding, and diligence. Proverbs 3:13-14 tells us, "Happy is the man who finds wisdom, and the man who gains understanding; for her proceeds are better than the profits of silver, and her gain than fine gold."

Improving grades requires a multi-faceted approach, combining practical strategies with spiritual grounding. With dedication, perseverance, and trust in God's plan, academic improvement is within reach. Remember, it's the journey and the lessons learned along the way that shape us, not just the final outcome. Lean on the Lord for strength, wisdom, and guidance, and let His love be the driving force behind every academic endeavor.

Edward D. Andrews

THE OUTSIDER 28 How Can I Cope with So Much Homework?

For many young individuals, the mere mention of the word "homework" evokes a sense of dread. The mountains of assignments, looming deadlines, and the challenge of balancing schoolwork with other life responsibilities can feel overwhelming. Yet, the Bible encourages us in Colossians 3:23, "Whatever you do, work at it with all your heart, as working for the Lord, not for human masters." So, how can you manage the daunting task of homework with a heart focused on honoring God?

The Purpose of Homework

Understanding the why behind homework can reshape our perspective.

Reinforcement of Knowledge: Homework serves to reinforce what was taught during class, aiding in the retention and application of knowledge.

Development of Discipline: Regular assignments help instill a sense of discipline and work ethic, virtues extolled in Scripture.

Preparation for Future Tasks: It's not just about the immediate subject at hand. Homework prepares students for higher education and future job responsibilities.

Practical Steps to Manage Homework Effectively

Establish a Routine:

Having a set time and place for homework creates a predictable pattern, making the task part of your daily rhythm. Ecclesiastes 3:1 reminds us, "There is a time for everything, and a season for every activity under the heavens."

Break Tasks into Manageable Portions:

Rather than viewing homework as one large, insurmountable task, break it down. Tackle one assignment or even one portion of an assignment at a time. Proverbs 24:27 advises, "Put your outdoor work in order and get your fields ready; after that, build your house."

Stay Organized:

Use planners, apps, or simple to-do lists to keep track of assignments. An organized approach can help prevent the stress of forgotten tasks or last-minute rushes.

Prioritize Assignments:

Identify which assignments are most urgent or carry the most weight for your grade. Tackle those tasks first, then move on to less pressing assignments.

Limit Distractions:

Find a quiet place to work, free from interruptions. This might mean turning off your phone or letting family members know you shouldn't be disturbed during homework time. Proverbs 4:25-26 says, "Let your eyes look straight ahead; fix your gaze directly before you. Give careful thought to the paths for your feet and be steadfast in all your ways."

Seek Help When Needed:

If a particular topic is challenging, don't hesitate to seek help. This could mean talking to a teacher, hiring a tutor, or joining a study group. Remember, James 1:5 tells us, "If any of you lacks wisdom, you should ask God, who gives generously to all without finding fault, and it will be given to you."

Spiritual Approaches to Cope with Homework Overload

Start with Prayer:

Before beginning your homework, take a moment to pray. Ask God for clarity, understanding, and the ability to focus on the task at hand.

Rest in God's Peace:

When you feel overwhelmed, take a short break and meditate on God's promises. Philippians 4:7 promises, "And the peace of God, which transcends all understanding, will guard your hearts and your minds in Christ Jesus."

Remember Your Worth:

Your value isn't solely based on academic achievements. God values you for who you are in Him. While it's crucial to strive for excellence, remember Romans 8:38-39, "For I am convinced that neither death nor life, neither angels nor demons, neither the present nor the future, nor any powers, neither height nor depth, nor anything else in all creation, will be able to separate us from the love of God that is in Christ Jesus our Lord."

Seek Balance:

While schoolwork is essential, it's equally crucial to maintain a balance in life. Make time for relaxation, hobbies, and spiritual activities. In Mark 6:31, Jesus told His disciples, "Come with me by yourselves to a quiet place and get some rest," emphasizing the importance of balance in our lives.

Tackling a pile of homework might feel like facing a giant at times. Yet, with practical strategies and a heart centered on God, you can conquer each task with confidence and grace. As you journey through these formative years, lean on God's strength, and remember that every challenge you face is an opportunity to grow both academically and spiritually.

THE OUTSIDER 29 How Can I Deal with Difficult Teachers?

Every student, at some point in their academic journey, encounters a teacher whom they find challenging. Whether it's due to perceived unfairness, a communication gap, or personal differences, difficult teacher-student relationships can significantly affect a student's emotional well-being and academic performance. Nevertheless, the Bible imparts wisdom on how to interact with those in positions of authority and offers guidance for such situations.

Understanding the Teacher's Perspective

Before diving into strategies, it's essential to grasp a broader view:

Professional Pressure: Teachers often work under significant pressure to meet educational standards, which can manifest in their interactions with students.

Personal Lives: Like everyone, teachers have personal lives filled with challenges. Sometimes personal struggles can unintentionally spill into the classroom.

Varied Student Personalities: Teachers engage with a multitude of personalities daily. Adapting to each student's unique needs can be taxing.

Scriptural Foundations for Interactions

Respect for Authority: Romans 13:1 reminds us, "Let everyone be subject to the governing authorities, for there is no authority except that which God has established." This principle extends to all figures of authority in our lives, including teachers.

Love and Understanding: Colossians 3:12 encourages, "Therefore, as God's chosen people, holy and dearly loved, clothe yourselves with compassion, kindness, humility, gentleness, and patience." Applying this towards teachers can transform interactions.

Practical Steps to Navigating Difficult Teacher Relationships

Open Communication:

Schedule a private meeting with the teacher to express your concerns. Approach the conversation with humility, seeking to understand rather than confront.

Be Proactive:

Rather than waiting for issues to escalate, be proactive in your studies. Seek clarification on assignments or feedback to prevent misunderstandings.

Stay Respectful:

Even if you disagree with a teacher, maintain a respectful tone. Proverbs 15:1 says, "A gentle answer turns away wrath, but a harsh word stirs up anger."

Seek Counsel:

Discuss your challenges with a guidance counselor or trusted adult. They might provide insights or mediate if necessary.

Stay Dedicated to Your Work:

Your primary responsibility as a student is to learn. Even in challenging circumstances, stay committed to your studies. Galatians 6:9 encourages, "Let us not become weary in doing good, for at the proper time we will reap a harvest if we do not give up."

Pray for Your Teacher:

Prayer can change hearts and situations. Lift up your teacher in prayer, asking God to grant both of you understanding and harmony. James 5:16 reminds us, "The prayer of a righteous person is powerful and effective."

Strategies to Cultivate a Positive Classroom Experience

Active Participation:

Engage actively in class. Your genuine interest might bridge communication gaps.

Empathy:

Put yourself in the teacher's shoes. Understanding their perspective can change your view of the situation.

Develop Resilience:

Every challenging situation is an opportunity for growth. Developing resilience now will benefit you in future challenges. Romans 5:3-4 says, "Not only so, but we also glory in our sufferings, because we know that suffering produces perseverance; perseverance, character; and character, hope."

Seek Peer Support:

Share your feelings with close friends. They might offer fresh perspectives, coping strategies, or even share similar experiences, reminding you that you're not alone.

Consider Extracurricular Assistance:

If academic friction is the primary issue, consider seeking outside help like tutoring to grasp the subject better. This step can relieve some of the classroom tension.

Navigating difficult relationships is a part of life, and the classroom is no exception. However, by turning to Scripture and implementing wise strategies, you can transform challenges into growth opportunities. Remember, the ultimate goal is not just academic success, but also cultivating Christ-like character in every situation. Every interaction, even the challenging ones, is an opportunity to reflect God's love and grace.

SECTION 5 Surviving Who I Am

Edward D. Andrews

THE OUTSIDER 30 Why Do I Procrastinate?

Procrastination, the act of delaying or postponing tasks, is a common struggle among young people. The reasons for this behavior are multifaceted, with influences spanning personal, psychological, and spiritual realms. While it's often dismissed as mere laziness, the roots of procrastination often run much deeper.

The Nature of Procrastination

Before we delve into the why, let's clarify what procrastination is not:

Simple Laziness: While it may seem like pure laziness, procrastination is often a complex response to various emotions and challenges.

Intentional Neglect: Procrastinators usually have every intention of completing the task, just "later."

Spiritual and Scriptural Insight on Delay

The Bible offers insights on laziness and delay. Proverbs 24:33-34 states, "A little sleep, a little slumber, a little folding of the hands to rest, and poverty will come upon you like a robber, and want like an armed man." God's Word encourages diligence and warns against the pitfalls of persistent delay.

Root Causes of Procrastination

Fear of Failure:

One of the most common reasons young people procrastinate is the fear of failure. The pressure to succeed and the potential for disappointment can paralyze an individual, making delay seem preferable to potential failure.

Perfectionism:

This is closely tied to the fear of failure. Many young people feel that if they can't complete a task perfectly, it's better not to start.

Decisional Procrastination:

At times, one might delay because they're uncertain about the best course of action. This type of procrastination is rooted in indecision.

Task Aversion:

Simply disliking a task can lead to procrastination. It's natural to want to avoid unpleasant activities.

Lack of Discipline or Self-Control:

Galatians 5:22-23 speaks of the fruit of the Spirit, one of which is self-control. Young people who haven't cultivated this trait might struggle with procrastination.

Coping with Overwhelm:

In a world that constantly demands attention, it's easy to feel overwhelmed. Procrastination can be a misguided attempt to manage these feelings.

Strategies to Overcome Procrastination

Start Small:

The journey of a thousand miles begins with a single step. By breaking tasks into smaller, manageable parts, the overall job becomes less intimidating.

Set Clear Goals:

Clearly defined goals with tangible rewards can serve as motivation. Consider Philippians 3:14, "I press on toward the goal to win the prize for which God has called me heavenward in Christ Jesus."

Establish a Routine:

Consistency can combat procrastination. Dedicate specific times for specific tasks, creating a routine that becomes a natural part of your day.

Limit Distractions:

In an age of constant digital interruptions, it's crucial to create a focused environment. This might mean turning off notifications, creating a dedicated workspace, or setting specific 'deep work' periods.

Seek Accountability:

Share your goals with a trusted friend or family member who can check on your progress. Accountability can be a powerful motivator.

Pray for Strength and Discipline:

Remember, God's strength is made perfect in our weakness (2 Corinthians 12:9). Regularly seek His guidance and strength in your endeavors.

Reframe Your Mindset:

Instead of viewing tasks as burdens, see them as opportunities for growth, learning, or service.

Visualize the End Result:

Thinking about the satisfaction or relief once a task is done can be a potent motivator. It gives a clearer perspective on the rewards of diligence.

Grace in the Face of Procrastination

While the Bible encourages diligence, it also offers grace for our shortcomings. Proverbs 19:21 says, "Many are the plans in a person's heart, but it is the Lord's purpose that prevails."

Remember, it's crucial not to be too hard on yourself. Everyone, at some point, struggles with procrastination. The key is to recognize it, understand its roots, and take proactive steps towards overcoming it. By seeking God's guidance and applying practical strategies, young people can conquer the habit of delay and step into a more productive, purpose-filled life.

THE OUTSIDER 31 Why Do I Focus on My Looks So Much?

In an age where image seems to be everything, it's not surprising that young people find themselves preoccupied with their physical appearance. The societal pressures to conform to certain beauty standards, combined with the personal desire to be accepted and valued, can cause a disproportionate emphasis on looks. But why is this emphasis so pronounced, especially among teenagers and young adults?

The Lens of Scripture

The Bible acknowledges the appeal of physical beauty but also offers a balanced perspective. Proverbs 31:30 reminds us, "Charm is deceptive, and beauty is fleeting; but a woman who fears the Lord is to be praised." This verse encapsulates the transient nature of physical beauty and underscores the value of spiritual qualities.

Understanding the Obsession with Looks

Societal Influences:

The society we live in is saturated with images of 'perfect' bodies, flawless skin, and impeccable fashion. These images, perpetuated by media, advertisements, and even social platforms, can lead to an internalized standard of beauty that's often unrealistic.

Peer Pressure and the Desire for Acceptance:

The teenage years are characterized by a longing for acceptance and the desire to 'fit in.' Physical appearance can become a ticket to acceptance, especially if one's peers value it highly.

Developmental Factors:

Adolescence is a time of rapid physical change. The natural preoccupation with body image during this phase can be traced back to the developmental need to establish a personal identity.

Effects of Social Media:

Platforms like Instagram, Snapchat, and TikTok focus heavily on visuals, further amplifying the importance of appearance. The comparison trap – juxtaposing one's own life and looks with the filtered realities of others – is a real and present danger.

Intrinsic Self-worth and Validation Seeking:

When young people derive their worth from external sources, such as compliments or 'likes' on a photo, they're on shaky ground. This dependency on external validation can be a significant driver for the obsession with looks.

Fear of Rejection:

For many, the underlying fear is rejection. There's a belief that looking a certain way reduces the risk of being rejected or overlooked.

Steps Towards a Healthier Perspective

Recognize the Deception of Media:

It's crucial to understand that many images in the media are altered. What's portrayed as 'real' is often a result of digital enhancements.

Dive into the Word:

Encourage regular engagement with Scripture. Psalm 139:14 declares, "I praise you because I am fearfully and wonderfully made;

your works are wonderful, I know that full well." This verse can be a foundational truth for self-worth.

Cultivate Inner Beauty:

1 Peter 3:3-4 offers this counsel, "Your beauty should not come from outward adornment... Rather, it should be that of your inner self, the unfading beauty of a gentle and quiet spirit, which is of great worth in God's sight." Cultivating qualities like kindness, compassion, and humility brings lasting beauty.

Seek Supportive Communities:

Finding and being part of a community that values inner qualities can offer respite from the external pressures of the world.

Limit Social Media Intake:

Reducing time spent on visual-focused social platforms can alleviate the constant pressure to compare.

Engage in Reflective Practices:

Prayer, journaling, and meditation can help in fostering a deeper self-understanding and a connection with God.

Talk About It:

Open dialogue with trusted individuals, be it parents, mentors, or counselors, can provide clarity, support, and perspective.

Re-define Beauty:

Encourage young people to create their own definition of beauty, one that encompasses both inner and outer qualities.

While it's natural to appreciate and take care of our physical appearance, the excessive focus on looks can be detrimental. The key lies in understanding the underlying reasons for this preoccupation and realigning one's perspective with God's truth. By valuing the inner person and recognizing the transient nature of physical beauty, young people can navigate these formative years with confidence and grace.

THE OUTSIDER 32 I Feel Like Ending It All

[Note: The topic of suicidal ideation is a grave one. If someone you know is struggling with these thoughts, it is crucial to seek immediate professional help.]

The weight of life can sometimes become so unbearable that a person may think of escaping it all. The feelings of despair, hopelessness, and pain may seem endless, pushing someone to the edge, believing that the only way out is to end their life. It's a tragic mindset, and understanding it is crucial not just for those feeling this way but also for those around them.

Unraveling the Why

Inherent Value in Every Life:

Scripture consistently emphasizes the inherent value of every individual. From the moment of conception, every person is unique, bearing the image of God (Genesis 1:27). No circumstance or struggle can diminish this inherent worth.

Reasons Behind Suicidal Thoughts:

Depression and Mental Illness:

Depression is one of the most common mental health issues that can lead to suicidal ideation. The intense feelings of sadness, hopelessness, and numbness can make life seem unbearable.

Traumatic Events:

Events like the loss of a loved one, abuse, or any form of trauma can be triggers.

Overwhelming Pressure:

This could stem from academic pressures, issues at home, or bullying.

Chemical Imbalance:

Certain neurological conditions caused by chemical imbalances can lead to such extreme thoughts.

Feeling Isolated or Misunderstood:

The feeling of being alone or misunderstood can amplify negative thoughts.

Scriptural Insights on Despair:

The Bible doesn't shy away from characters who have faced deep despair. Elijah, after a significant victory, found himself in the wilderness asking God to take his life (1 Kings 19:4). Jonah, after successfully prophesying to Nineveh, wished to die out of frustration and anger (Jonah 4:3). These instances show that even God's servants aren't immune to feelings of hopelessness. But in each case, God intervenes, providing comfort, correction, and direction.

Moving from Despair to Hope

Immediate Intervention is Crucial:

If you or someone you know is struggling with suicidal thoughts, seeking immediate professional help is vital. The gravity of this situation should never be underestimated.

Strengthening Spiritual Foundations:

Dive deep into God's Word and His promises. Scriptures such as Psalm 34:18, which says, "The Lord is close to the brokenhearted and saves those who are crushed in spirit," can be of comfort.

Building a Support System:

Having trusted individuals, whether they're friends, family, or mentors, can be a lifeline. These individuals can provide emotional support, prayer, and can help ensure that the struggling person gets professional help.

Engage in Therapeutic Practices:

Christian counseling, prayer, and journaling can help process feelings and emotions.

Limiting Negative Influences:

Reducing exposure to negative influences, whether they're toxic relationships or harmful online content, can make a difference.

Remember the Temporality of Struggles:

While the pain may seem endless, it's crucial to remember that many struggles are temporary.

The Church's Role

The church community can play a vital role in providing support. By fostering an environment where individuals feel safe sharing their struggles, by offering counseling resources, and by continually pointing to the hope found in Christ, the church can be a refuge.

Feelings of hopelessness and the thought of ending it all are serious. These feelings reflect deep pain and despair. However, it's essential to remember that God cares deeply for each individual and that He offers hope and healing. Through a combination of spiritual, emotional, and professional support, one can find their way back from the edge and experience a renewed sense of purpose and joy. If you or someone you know is struggling, please reach out for help immediately. God's love and the love of the community await you.

Edward D. Andrews

THE OUTSIDER 33 Why Do I Cut Myself?

[Note: Self-harm is a grave concern. If someone is struggling with self-harm or suicidal thoughts, immediate professional help is essential.]

The act of cutting oneself or engaging in other forms of self-harm is a manifestation of deeper emotional and psychological pain. Many young people wrestle with these tendencies, often doing so in secret. Understanding the reasons behind self-harm can pave the way for healing and restoration.

Understanding the Act of Cutting

Defining Self-Harm:

Self-harm refers to any deliberate action taken to harm oneself without the actual intention of ending one's life. Cutting is one of the most common forms, but burning, biting, hitting, or any other form of self-inflicted pain falls under this umbrella.

Reasons Behind Cutting:

1. **Emotional Release:** Some describe the act of cutting as a way to release overwhelming emotions. The physical pain momentarily distracts from emotional pain.
2. **Regaining Control:** Life's circumstances can make young people feel out of control. Cutting can be a way to exert control over at least one aspect of their lives.
3. **Self-Punishment:** Some use cutting as a form of self-punishment, often rooted in feelings of guilt or unworthiness.
4. **Expressing Inner Turmoil:** For those who find it hard to communicate their emotions verbally, self-harm can be a cry for help, signaling to others that they are in distress.

Biblical Perspective on Self-Worth:

Scripture consistently emphasizes our intrinsic worth and value in God's eyes. Psalm 139:14 states, "I praise you because I am fearfully and wonderfully made." Every individual is created with purpose and love by God. The act of self-harm is contrary to the inherent value that each person holds.

From Despair to Hope: Pathways to Healing

Recognizing the Need for Help:

Admitting the problem is the first step. Accepting that you need assistance and support to overcome this challenge is crucial.

Seeking Professional Counseling:

A Christian counselor can provide guidance, coping mechanisms, and biblical insight. They can help address the root causes of the pain and offer therapeutic techniques.

Engaging in Alternative Coping Mechanisms:

1. **Journaling:** Writing down feelings can provide an emotional outlet.
2. **Art:** Drawing, painting, or any other form of art can be therapeutic.
3. **Prayer:** Direct communication with God can bring solace and strength.

Building a Support System:

Surrounding oneself with understanding friends, mentors, and family members who can offer support, listen, and pray can make a profound difference.

Avoiding Triggers:

Certain situations, feelings, or even people might trigger the urge to self-harm. Recognizing and avoiding these can be a protective measure.

Resting in God's Promises:

God promises to be near the broken-hearted (Psalm 34:18). Relying on His strength, seeking His presence through prayer, and immersing oneself in Scripture can offer solace.

The Church and Community's Role

1. **Education**: Churches should educate their members about the signs of self-harm and the reasons behind it.
2. **Foster Safe Spaces**: Creating an environment where young people can share without judgment is crucial.
3. **Professional Resources**: Churches can offer resources or referrals for professional Christian counseling.
4. **Prayer and Support**: Regularly uplifting the struggling individuals in prayer and letting them know they are loved and cared for can make a difference.

Self-harm is a cry of deep emotional distress. The act of cutting, though a manifestation of internal pain, doesn't offer a true solution or lasting relief. With the right support, both from a spiritual and psychological perspective, healing is attainable. God's unwavering love, the support of the community, and professional intervention can guide the individual from the depths of despair to a place of hope and restoration. If you or someone you know is struggling with self-harm, please reach out for help immediately. Your life has immeasurable value in the eyes of God.

THE OUTSIDER 34 Are Tattoos Really that Bad?

In contemporary culture, tattoos have grown increasingly popular, especially among young people. They can be a form of self-expression, a memorial for significant life events, or even an artistic statement. However, when viewed from a conservative Christian lens, the decision to get a tattoo may come with additional considerations. Let's delve into both the cultural and biblical perspectives on tattoos.

Tattoos: A Historical and Cultural Overview

The History of Tattoos:

Tattooing is an ancient practice, spanning various cultures and millennia. From the tribes of Polynesia to the ancient Egyptians, tattoos have served as rites of passage, marks of status, or symbols of religious devotion.

Modern-Day Acceptance:

Today, tattoos have largely shifted from taboo to mainstream in many cultures worldwide. For many, they symbolize personal growth, memorialize loved ones, or showcase artistic inclinations.

Biblical Perspectives on Tattoos

The Bible isn't silent about the matter of marking one's body. However, one must exercise caution when interpreting and applying these passages, ensuring they are understood in their proper context.

Leviticus 19:28: This is the most commonly cited verse regarding tattoos: "You shall not make any cuts on your body for the dead or tattoo yourselves: I am the Lord." While this command was given to the Israelites and was part of the Old Testament Law, it raises questions about its applicability to Christians today.

New Testament Silence: The New Testament does not specifically address the issue of tattoos. Instead, the emphasis is often on the inner character and the heart's condition rather than external appearances.

Moral and Ethical Considerations:

1. **Intention and Motivation**: Why do you want a tattoo? Is it to fit in, rebel, or commemorate something meaningful? Evaluating the intent is vital before making a permanent decision.

2. **The Temple of the Holy Spirit**: 1 Corinthians 6:19-20 reminds us that our bodies are temples of the Holy Spirit. Any modifications to our bodies, including tattoos, should be considered in this light.

3. **Offending Others**: Romans 14 speaks about not causing others to stumble. If getting a tattoo might hurt your testimony or relationships, especially within a conservative community, it's worth reconsidering.

Theological Implications:

1. **Grace versus Law**: Christians live under grace and are not bound by the Old Testament Law (Romans 6:14). However, the principles behind the Law, including the reasons for certain prohibitions, can still offer wisdom.

2. **Conformity to the World**: Romans 12:2 warns against conforming to the world. It's essential to discern if the desire for a tattoo stems from godly motives or worldly influences.

3. **Permanence and Future Regret**: The permanence of tattoos means they're not a decision to be made lightly. Just as with any lifelong decision, seek counsel, pray, and reflect.

Practical Considerations

1. **Health and Safety**: Ensure that the tattoo parlor follows all health regulations to avoid infections or diseases.

2. **Future Implications**: Consider potential future ramifications, such as job prospects or changing personal beliefs.
3. **Artistic Value and Quality**: If one decides to get a tattoo, ensuring its artistic quality can prevent future regrets.

The decision to get a tattoo, especially from a conservative Christian perspective, is multifaceted. While the Bible does not outright ban the practice for New Testament believers, it does offer guiding principles about how we should view our bodies and the motives behind our decisions. It's crucial to approach the topic with an open heart, seeking God's wisdom and guidance. Every individual must weigh the cultural, personal, and biblical implications and arrive at a decision that they believe honors God and aligns with their convictions. Whether one decides to get a tattoo or refrain, it should be a decision made with maturity, thoughtfulness, and prayer.

Edward D. Andrews

THE OUTSIDER 35 Is Cursing Really That Bad?

In an era where language and its boundaries are continuously shifting, many young people find themselves pondering the real implications of their words. Cursing, in particular, stands as a controversial topic, especially when viewed from a conservative Christian standpoint. The central question becomes: "Is cursing really that bad?" To address this, we need to explore both the cultural and biblical perspectives on the use of profane language.

Understanding Cursing: A Cultural Perspective

Evolution of Language: Language is dynamic. What was considered taboo or offensive a few decades ago might be commonly used today. Younger generations, with their novel slang and expressions, often find themselves at odds with older generations about what is deemed acceptable speech.

Social Contexts: In some circles, cursing can be seen as a form of bonding or a way to emphasize feelings. Among friends, what might be considered a curse word can be taken as a joke or term of endearment. However, in more formal settings, cursing can be viewed as disrespectful or unprofessional.

The Impact on Listener: Regardless of intent, words have the power to affect listeners. What might not offend one person could deeply hurt another. Understanding one's audience is crucial.

Biblical Perspectives on Cursing

The Power of the Tongue:

Scripture places significant emphasis on the power of speech. Proverbs 18:21 states, *"Death and life are in the power of the tongue, and those who love it will eat its fruits."* Words can build up or tear down, bless or curse.

Wholesome Talk:

Ephesians 4:29 instructs, *"Let no corrupting talk come out of your mouths, but only such as is good for building up, as fits the occasion, that it may give grace to those who hear."* This verse challenges believers to use their words for edification, not destruction.

Reflecting the Heart:

Jesus pointed out that our words are a reflection of our hearts. In Matthew 12:34, He said, *"For out of the abundance of the heart the mouth speaks."* If one is frequently cursing, it might be a sign of underlying heart issues.

God's Name in Vain:

One of the Ten Commandments specifically addresses the misuse of God's name (Exodus 20:7). This form of cursing—using God's name flippantly or as a swear word—is directly confronted in Scripture.

Moral and Ethical Considerations

1. **Respect for Others**: Even if cursing is a common part of one's vernacular, it's essential to respect the feelings and beliefs of others. Avoiding profanity in mixed company shows consideration and maturity.

2. **Personal Reputation**: Like it or not, people often judge others by how they speak. Cursing can leave an impression of impulsiveness, immaturity, or a lack of self-control.

3. **Desensitization**: Regularly using or hearing curse words can desensitize individuals to their impact. Over time, stronger and more offensive words might be needed to convey the same emotion, leading to even cruder language.

Theological Implications

1. **Being Set Apart:** Christians are called to be "in the world, not of the world" (John 17:16). This distinction also applies to speech. By refraining from cursing, believers can stand out and reflect Christ in their conversations.

2. **Guarding the Heart:** As previously mentioned, frequent cursing might indicate a deeper issue of the heart. Regular self-reflection and repentance are essential for spiritual growth.

3. **Witnessing Opportunities:** Clean speech can open doors for spiritual conversations. When others notice a lack of profanity, it can lead to questions about one's faith and beliefs.

From a conservative Christian perspective, the issue of cursing is not merely about cultural shifts or personal freedom. It delves into the deeper realms of respect, self-control, and sanctification. The Bible underscores the immense power and responsibility tied to speech. As young individuals navigate the complexities of coming-of-age in today's world, understanding the weight of words and striving to use them wisely can serve as a beacon, guiding their interactions and relationships. The choice to refrain from cursing can be a testament to one's faith, a reflection of the heart's condition, and a powerful tool for witness in a world increasingly desensitized to the potency of words.

THE OUTSIDER 36 Is Alcohol Really That Bad?

For many young people navigating the tumultuous waters of adolescence and young adulthood, the allure of alcohol beckons as both a rite of passage and a cultural mainstay. However, the question lingers: "Is alcohol really that bad?" From the gatherings where it's served to the movies that glamorize its effects, alcohol's presence is pervasive. Yet, its consequences, when abused, can be devastating. As we tackle this topic, we'll delve into its cultural, biological, moral, and spiritual dimensions from a conservative Christian standpoint.

Understanding Alcohol: A Cultural Lens

Social Rituals: Alcohol has been part of human society for centuries. In many cultures, it's seen as a symbol of celebration, hospitality, or camaraderie. This widespread acceptance can often make abstaining or questioning alcohol's role seem out of place.

Media Influence: Movies, music, and TV often glamorize alcohol consumption. Scenes of parties, toasts, and relaxation frequently feature alcohol as the main prop, giving young people a skewed perception of its role and effects.

The Biological Impacts of Alcohol

The Developing Brain: Research indicates that the human brain continues to develop well into the mid-20s. Alcohol can adversely affect this development, leading to issues in decision-making, impulse control, and memory.

Dependency and Addiction: Some individuals are more genetically predisposed to alcohol addiction than others. The earlier one starts drinking, the higher the chances of developing alcohol-related problems later in life.

Physical Health: Excessive alcohol consumption has been linked to liver diseases, digestive problems, heart complications, and more. It weakens the immune system and can be a factor in accidents due to impaired judgment and motor functions.

Mental Health: Alcohol can exacerbate symptoms of depression and anxiety. Many believe it offers relief, but it can end up creating a vicious cycle of dependence and worsening mental health issues.

Moral and Ethical Considerations

Impaired Judgment: Under the influence, individuals might make decisions they'd typically avoid, leading to regrettable actions and consequences.

Influence on Others: Peer pressure can lead some to overconsume or try alcohol before they're legally allowed. One's choices can affect and even endanger peers.

Personal Responsibility: Engaging with alcohol requires a level of responsibility. This includes understanding personal limits and ensuring safety for oneself and others.

Biblical Insights on Alcohol

Not Explicitly Forbidden, But...: The Bible doesn't categorically forbid drinking alcohol. Jesus turned water into wine at the Cana wedding (John 2:1-11). However, Scripture is clear about drunkenness. Ephesians 5:18 says, *"Do not get drunk on wine, which leads to debauchery."*

A Matter of Conscience and Witness:

Romans 14 discusses the matter of personal conscience in issues like food and drink. It emphasizes not causing others to stumble. If consuming alcohol might lead someone else astray or weaken their faith, it's advised to abstain.

Wisdom and Moderation: Proverbs 20:1 warns, *"Wine is a mocker, strong drink is raging: and whosoever is deceived thereby is not wise."* Scripture encourages wisdom and discernment in all things, including alcohol consumption.

The Spiritual Ramifications

Body as a Temple: 1 Corinthians 6:19-20 reminds believers that their bodies are temples of the Holy Spirit. What one ingests or how one treats their body has spiritual implications.

Potential for Idolatry: Anything, including alcohol, can become an idol if it takes precedence over God in one's life or is relied upon for comfort, escape, or identity.

Seeking True Joy: While many turn to alcohol for temporary joy or relief, the Bible offers a more profound, lasting joy through the Holy Spirit (Galatians 5:22-23).

From a conservative Christian perspective, the issue isn't about the mere act of consuming alcohol but the motivations, implications, and potential consequences surrounding it. While society might offer a laissez-faire attitude towards drinking, Christians are urged to approach the matter with prudence, knowledge, and a deep concern for the spiritual and physical well-being of themselves and others. In a world where the lines of moderation and excess often blur, discernment becomes the compass, guiding choices and influencing actions in light of a faith that values the sanctity of the body, mind, and spirit.

Edward D. Andrews

THE OUTSIDER 37 Is Anger Really That Bad?

The tumult of adolescence and early adulthood is replete with intense emotions, chief among them being anger. Whether it's an outburst at a parent, a feud with a friend, or simmering resentment over perceived slights, anger is an emotion familiar to all, yet deeply misunderstood. Let's demystify this powerful emotion, explore its origins, its potential impact, and how it can be navigated from a conservative Christian perspective.

Understanding Anger: A Natural Emotion

The Biological Response: Anger is a natural human emotion, often triggered as a defense mechanism against threats, whether real or perceived. Biologically, it causes the release of adrenaline, preparing the body for the "fight or flight" response.

The Spectrum of Anger: Anger varies in intensity from mild irritation to intense fury and rage. Understanding the differences is crucial for addressing and managing this emotion.

When Anger Becomes Sinful: Ephesians 4:26 says, *"Be angry, and do not sin."* This suggests that anger, in itself, isn't the issue; it's how one responds or acts upon it.

The Causes of Anger in Young People

Unresolved Past Traumas: Past hurts, whether emotional, physical, or psychological, can manifest as anger if not dealt with appropriately.

Perceived Injustices: When young individuals feel mistreated or that life is unfair, anger can be a natural response.

Pressure and Stress: The pressures of school, relationships, and future uncertainties can be overwhelming, leading to anger outbursts.

Unmet Expectations: Disappointments, whether from failed goals, relationships, or personal expectations, can cause deep-seated anger.

The Consequences of Unchecked Anger

Physical Health: Chronic anger can lead to problems like high blood pressure, heart disease, and weakened immune systems.

Mental Health: Continual anger can increase the risk of depression, anxiety, and other mood disorders.

Relationships: Unchecked anger can strain relationships, leading to isolation, misunderstandings, and deep-seated resentments.

Spiritual Well-being: Allowing anger to control one's actions can distance a person from God and impede spiritual growth.

Biblical Insights on Anger

Righteous Anger vs. Sinful Anger: Jesus displayed anger when he cleansed the temple (John 2:13-16). His anger was directed at the injustice and misuse of God's house. This differentiates righteous anger, which is directed at sin and injustice, from sinful anger, which is self-centered and malicious.

The Warning against Anger: Proverbs 29:22 says, *"An angry person stirs up conflict, and a hot-tempered person commits many sins."* Scripture acknowledges the destructive nature of unchecked anger.

Managing and Responding to Anger

Self-Reflection: Recognize the triggers. Understand what ignites anger and avoid or address these situations with preparedness.

Seek Counsel: James 1:19 advises, *"Let every person be quick to listen, slow to speak, slow to anger."* Speaking to trusted individuals about feelings can provide clarity and perspective.

Prayer and Meditation: Philippians 4:6-7 speaks of bringing all anxieties to God in prayer. When anger threatens to overwhelm, seeking God's peace can be the calming balm.

Positive Outlets: Physical activities, like sports or even a brisk walk, can help dissipate the adrenaline rush of anger. Creative expressions, like writing or art, can be therapeutic.

Seek Professional Help: When anger becomes uncontrollable, seeking therapy or counseling is crucial. It's a sign of strength, not weakness.

The Role of Forgiveness:

Jesus' teaching in Matthew 18:21-22 underscores the importance of forgiveness. Holding onto grudges and resentments only fuels anger. True liberation comes from forgiving, even if it seems undeserved.

In the journey of understanding and navigating anger, the key takeaway is that anger, in itself, isn't inherently bad. It becomes problematic when it leads to sin or is expressed harmfully. Through introspection, counsel, prayer, and proactive steps, young individuals can manage their anger in ways that align with Christian values, ensuring that their reactions don't lead them astray but bring them closer to the love and wisdom of God.

THE OUTSIDER 38 How Can I Recover from My Mistakes?

Everyone, at some point in their lives, grapples with mistakes – both small and large, inconsequential and life-changing. Mistakes can leave deep scars, not just in the external circumstances of our lives but more crucially, within the recesses of our soul. Yet, within the Christian framework, mistakes are not dead-ends; they can be springboards to spiritual growth, deeper self-awareness, and a richer relationship with God. For young individuals navigating the complexities of adolescence and young adulthood, understanding how to recover from mistakes is invaluable.

The Nature of Mistakes

What Constitutes a Mistake? A mistake is an action or judgment that is misguided or wrong. It can stem from ignorance, oversight, poor decision-making, or even willful rebellion.

Why Do We Make Mistakes? Romans 3:23 says, *"for all have sinned and fall short of the glory of God."* This innate human imperfection makes us prone to errors.

The Emotional Aftermath of Mistakes Feelings of guilt, shame, regret, and self-reproach often accompany mistakes. These emotions, while uncomfortable, can be constructive if channeled correctly.

The Redemptive Power of Mistakes

Mistakes as Learning Opportunities: Every error offers a lesson. It reveals areas of growth, highlights vulnerabilities, and teaches resilience.

Mistakes and Personal Growth: Challenges shape character. Recovering from a mistake can strengthen perseverance, humility, and self-awareness.

Spiritual Deepening Through Mistakes: Mistakes remind us of our dependence on God. They can foster a deeper relationship with Him, as we recognize our frailty and His sufficiency.

Practical Steps to Recovery

Acknowledgment and Acceptance: The first step in recovery is acknowledging the mistake. Psalms 32:5 says, *"I acknowledged my sin to you, and I did not cover my iniquity."* God honors a contrite heart that accepts responsibility.

Seeking Forgiveness: Whether it's God's forgiveness through prayer or seeking pardon from those wronged, this step is pivotal. 1 John 1:9 promises, *"If we confess our sins, he is faithful and just to forgive us our sins and to cleanse us from all unrighteousness."*

Restitution Where Possible: Wherever feasible, take steps to rectify the mistake. This might involve mending relationships, repaying debts, or any other action that restores balance.

Learning and Moving Forward: Post-reflection, discern the lessons the mistake has offered. Implement strategies or behavioral changes to prevent recurrence.

Seek Support: Speak to mentors, trusted friends, or counselors who can provide guidance, accountability, and encouragement. Proverbs 11:14 speaks of the wisdom in seeking counsel.

Embrace God's Grace: Remember Romans 8:1, *"There is therefore now no condemnation for those who are in Christ Jesus."* God's grace covers every mistake.

Developing a Resilient Mindset

Shifting from Shame to Grace: Instead of wallowing in self-condemnation, focus on God's unending grace and mercy.

Reframing the Narrative: See mistakes not as defining moments but as parts of a larger narrative of growth and spiritual maturity.

Remember Past Overcomings: Recall past instances where you've overcome challenges. This boosts confidence and resilience.

Avoiding Future Mistakes

Prayerful Decision Making: Before making decisions, especially pivotal ones, seek God's guidance through prayer.

Accountability Partners: Having someone to share struggles and victories with can prevent potential pitfalls.

Regular Self-Reflection: Periodic introspection helps in identifying patterns or tendencies that lead to mistakes, offering a chance to proactively address them.

Mistakes, though painful, are not the end. In the grand tapestry of life, they are threads that add depth, character, and lessons. For a young individual, every mistake is an opportunity – to lean closer to God, to grow in wisdom, and to mold character. The journey of recovery from mistakes, undergirded by God's grace, is a transformative one, leading not to a dead-end but to brighter horizons of spiritual and personal growth.

Edward D. Andrews

SECTION 6 Surviving Recreation

THE OUTSIDER 39 What Are the Dangers of Gaming?

In the digital age, gaming has emerged as a dominant form of entertainment for millions worldwide. Many young people, including Christians, find solace, excitement, and camaraderie in the virtual worlds of video games. While gaming can offer a momentary escape from the pressures of life and even provide some cognitive benefits, there are undeniable dangers associated with excessive and unguarded gaming. In our journey of understanding these potential pitfalls, it is essential to approach the subject with a balanced perspective, discerning the line between harmless fun and harmful obsession.

Understanding the Appeal of Gaming

A Virtual Escape: Gaming provides an alternate reality where players can be heroes, embark on epic quests, and create their narratives.

Social Connection: Multiplayer online games foster a sense of community, allowing players to form friendships and work together towards shared objectives.

Cognitive and Skill Development: Games often challenge players' reflexes, decision-making skills, and strategic thinking.

The Underlying Dangers

1. **Addiction and Compulsive Gaming**: The most significant danger of gaming is its potential for addiction. Just like substances, games can stimulate the brain's reward centers, leading to a relentless desire for more. Proverbs 25:16 reminds us, *"If you find honey, eat just*

enough—too much of it, and you will vomit." The same principle applies to gaming.

2. Social Isolation: While games might offer a virtual community, they can lead to real-world isolation. The Bible emphasizes the importance of real human connection, as seen in Hebrews 10:25, *"not neglecting to meet together, as is the habit of some, but encouraging one another."*

3. Impact on Physical Health: Extended gaming sessions can lead to sedentary lifestyles, contributing to health issues like obesity, poor posture, and even vision problems.

4. Impact on Mental Health: Excessive gaming can exacerbate anxiety, depression, and stress, particularly if the games played are violent or intense.

5. Displacement of Time: Time spent on gaming can encroach upon time for essential activities like prayer, Scripture study, family interactions, and academic commitments. Ephesians 5:16 encourages believers to "make the best use of the time," a directive that becomes challenging when gaming dominates one's schedule.

6. Exposure to Inappropriate Content: Many games contain content that is inconsistent with Christian values, such as explicit violence, sexual themes, occult elements, and profanity. 1 Corinthians 15:33 cautions, *"Do not be deceived: 'Bad company ruins good morals.'"* The content consumed can influence one's thought patterns and behavior.

7. Financial Implications: Microtransactions, a business model where players can purchase virtual items with real money, can lead to significant financial drain, especially for impulsive or addicted gamers.

Guarding Against the Dangers

Set Clear Boundaries: Establish gaming limits in terms of duration and frequency. As the Psalmist writes, *"So teach us to number our days that we may get a heart of wisdom"* (Psalm 90:12). Time is precious; use it wisely.

Choose Games Wisely: Be discerning about the games you play. Avoid those with content that conflicts with Christian values.

Balanced Lifestyle: Ensure that gaming doesn't displace physical activity, social interaction, and other vital aspects of a balanced life.

Stay Connected in Real Life: While virtual friendships can be meaningful, they should not replace real-world connections. Maintain active participation in church, family gatherings, and community activities.

Seek Accountability: Share your gaming habits with a trusted friend or family member who can provide guidance and accountability.

While the world of gaming can be captivating, it is crucial to approach it with caution and wisdom. Remembering the Christian call to moderation, wisdom, and righteousness can guide young individuals in navigating the challenges of the gaming world. By setting boundaries, making discerning choices, and prioritizing real-world connections, young believers can enjoy gaming without compromising their spiritual, physical, or emotional well-being.

THE OUTSIDER 40 Why Is My Music Choices Important?

Music is a powerful medium that has a profound influence on the human soul. Throughout history, melodies, rhythms, and harmonies have captivated hearts and minds, serving as an expression of culture, emotion, and the human experience. For the young Christian navigating the complexities of adolescence and young adulthood, music often plays a central role in shaping identity, values, and emotions. Given its pervasive impact, the question arises: Why are my music choices important? Let's delve into this crucial topic with understanding, discernment, and a Biblical perspective.

The Power of Music

Emotional Resonance: Music taps into our emotions, often more deeply than words alone. A song can uplift, sadden, inspire, or even provoke anger. As Proverbs 23:7 notes, *"For as he thinks in his heart, so is he."* What we allow into our hearts impacts who we become.

Memory and Association: Songs have an uncanny ability to transport us back to specific moments in our lives, evoking vivid memories and associated feelings. They become soundtracks to our life's events.

Cultural Expression: Music often reflects societal values, norms, and beliefs. It can both shape and be shaped by the culture it emerges from.

Spiritual Impact: Throughout Scripture, music plays a significant role in worship, warfare, celebration, and lament. It's a tool for both expressing and shaping spiritual realities.

Dangers of Unwise Music Choices

Misaligned Values: Many popular songs promote values that directly oppose Christian teachings, such as materialism, lust, revenge, and pride. Romans 12:2 warns believers not to be conformed to this world but be transformed by renewing their minds.

Negative Emotional Influence: Some genres or songs, especially those that emphasize despair, anger, or hopelessness, can drag down our emotional state, leading to anxiety, depression, or aggression.

Desensitization: Continuous exposure to harmful content can desensitize us, making us more accepting of behaviors and values that we would otherwise reject.

Distraction from Spiritual Growth: Music that doesn't edify or draw us closer to God can act as a distraction, pulling our focus away from things of eternal significance.

Choosing Music with Wisdom

Assess the Lyrics: While a catchy beat can draw us in, it's essential to pay close attention to a song's lyrics. What messages are they conveying? Do they align with Biblical truth?

Recognize the Emotional Impact: After listening to a song or album, assess how you feel. Does the music encourage positive emotions like joy, peace, and love, or does it induce anger, sadness, or anxiety?

Seek Songs that Edify: Paul writes in Philippians 4:8, *"whatever is true, whatever is noble, whatever is right, whatever is pure, whatever is lovely, whatever is admirable—if anything is excellent or praiseworthy—think about such things."* Music should be no exception.

Limit Exposure: If you find that certain genres, artists, or songs pull you away from God or promote ungodly behaviors and values, it might be time to limit or eliminate your exposure to them.

Worship and Spiritual Songs: Engaging with Christian music or songs that promote Scriptural truths can be a source of encouragement, conviction, and growth. Ephesians 5:19 encourages believers to *"speak to one another with psalms, hymns, and songs from the Spirit."*

Seeking Godly Counsel: If you're unsure about your music choices, consult with mature believers, pastors, or trusted Christian friends. They can offer guidance and a fresh perspective.

Your music choices are a reflection of what you allow to influence your heart and mind. Just as we feed our bodies with physical food, the music we consume feeds our souls. In a world filled with various messages and values, it's paramount for young Christians to guard their hearts and minds, making music choices that align with the eternal truths of Scripture. By approaching music with discernment, wisdom, and a Christ-centered perspective, young believers can navigate the complex world of music, using it as a tool for growth, edification, and worship.

THE OUTSIDER 41 How Can I Show Balance When It Comes to Sports?

Sports are an integral part of many young people's lives. Whether it's playing on a school team, watching games with family and friends, or avidly following a favorite professional team, sports can bring excitement, discipline, and camaraderie. Yet, like many good things, it's possible for sports to occupy an undue place in our lives, overshadowing other priorities and even becoming an idol. As Christians, we're called to live balanced lives, ensuring that all our pursuits honor God. Let's delve into how you can demonstrate balance in your involvement and enthusiasm for sports.

Understanding the Value of Sports

Before we delve into finding balance, let's understand why sports matter:

Physical Fitness: Engaging in sports keeps the body healthy, fulfilling the Biblical principle found in 1 Corinthians 6:19-20, which reminds us that our bodies are temples of the Holy Spirit.

Discipline and Dedication: Training, practicing, and competing teach valuable life skills such as discipline, perseverance, and dedication.

Teamwork and Unity: Playing on a team fosters unity, cooperation, and mutual respect, reflecting the unity of the body of Christ.

Character Building: Winning and losing graciously, facing challenges, and adhering to rules shape our character.

Dangers of Imbalance

While sports offer many benefits, there are potential pitfalls if they aren't approached with a balanced perspective:

Neglecting Spiritual Priorities: When training sessions, games, or even watching sports dominate our schedules, we might neglect personal Bible study, prayer, or church attendance.

Identity Crisis: Tying our entire identity to being an athlete or fan can be problematic. Our primary identity should be as children of God.

Poor Sportsmanship: An obsessive desire to win might lead to poor sportsmanship, reflecting poorly on our Christian testimony.

Excessive Emphasis on Physical Appearance: Overemphasis on athletic physique might lead to vanity or body image issues.

Practical Steps to Achieve Balance

Set Clear Priorities: Establishing clear priorities ensures that sports don't overshadow spiritual, familial, and academic responsibilities. Matthew 6:33 encourages us to seek God's kingdom first.

Limit Watching or Playing Time: Determine in advance how many hours per week you'll dedicate to playing or watching sports. Be disciplined in sticking to this limit.

Incorporate God into Your Sport: You can offer prayers before games or even share your faith with teammates. See your involvement in sports as a mission field where you can shine Christ's light.

Seek Accountability: Share your goals for balance with a trusted friend, family member, or mentor who can help you stay on track.

Stay Connected to Spiritual Activities: Regardless of how busy your sports schedule becomes, commit to regular church attendance, Bible study, and prayer.

Cultivate Other Interests: Ensure that sports aren't your only hobby. Dive into other activities like reading, music, art, or volunteer work. This broadens your perspective and ensures a more rounded personality.

Address the Heart: Regularly assess your heart and motivations. Are you seeking glory for yourself, or do you see sports as a way to glorify God and cultivate the gifts He's given you?

Consult Scripture and Pray: When faced with decisions related to sports (e.g., joining a new team, trying out for a demanding position), seek God's guidance through Scripture and prayer.

Sports, when approached rightly, can be a beautiful expression of God-given talents, discipline, and teamwork. Yet, like all things, they require balance. As young Christians, ensuring that our involvement in sports doesn't overshadow our commitment to Christ is crucial. By setting clear priorities, staying connected to spiritual activities, and consistently assessing our hearts and motivations, we can enjoy the myriad benefits of sports while maintaining a steadfast and unwavering commitment to our Lord and Savior, Jesus Christ.

THE OUTSIDER 42 How Is Social Media Affecting Me?

In today's digital age, social media platforms such as Instagram, Facebook, Twitter, and Snapchat have become the mainstay of communication for young individuals. The alluring pull of these platforms has reshaped the way the youth converse, share, and perceive the world around them. Yet, as with all tools, social media can be a double-edged sword. It can either be a source of connection and enlightenment or a potential cause for anxiety, depression, and estrangement from reality. Let's embark on an in-depth exploration of how social media might be influencing you, its benefits and pitfalls, and how to navigate it from a conservative Christian perspective.

The Allure of Social Media

A Sense of Connection: Social media bridges distances, allowing for instant communication with peers, friends, and family regardless of geographic locations. It fosters a sense of belonging, a virtual space where sharing and interaction occur seamlessly.

Expression of Identity: Platforms allow users to craft and showcase their identity, be it through photos, status updates, or shared content. They offer a venue for self-expression and creativity.

Information and Awareness: Social media has made information dissemination swift. News, updates, and knowledge are shared in real-time, promoting awareness on global events.

Dangers and Pitfalls

Comparison Culture: As individuals share their 'highlight reels', it's easy to fall into the comparison trap, feeling that one's own life doesn't measure up to the idealized online lives of peers. This can lead to feelings of inadequacy, jealousy, and discontent.

Mental Health Concerns: Excessive use of social media has been linked to increased feelings of anxiety, depression, and loneliness. The quest for validation through likes, comments, and shares can become an unhealthy obsession.

Distorted Reality: What's shared on social media is often a curated version of reality. Yet, continuous exposure can lead to skewed perceptions, making it challenging to differentiate between the virtual and the real.

Loss of Privacy: Sharing personal information can lead to breaches in privacy and potential exposure to malicious intents. Personal details, once on the internet, can seldom be retracted completely.

Temptation and Spiritual Dangers: From unsavory content to cyberbullying, social media can expose young Christians to temptations and negative influences that can be spiritually damaging.

Navigating Social Media with Wisdom

Set Boundaries: Establish designated times to check social media. Avoid the compulsive need to check notifications incessantly. Make conscious efforts to unplug, dedicating time for offline activities.

Guard Your Heart: As Proverbs 4:23 reminds us, "Guard your heart above all else, for it determines the course of your life." Be discerning about the content you consume and share. Unfollow accounts or pages that stir negative emotions or temptations.

Seek Genuine Connections: Prioritize face-to-face interactions. While online friends can be valuable, there's a depth to offline relationships that virtual connections often lack.

Practice Contentment: Remember Philippians 4:11-13, where Paul speaks of learning to be content in all situations. Your worth is not determined by online validation but by your identity in Christ.

Engage in Constructive Activities: Instead of passive consumption, use social media for constructive activities such as sharing Scripture, joining Christian groups, or engaging in discussions that edify.

Pray for Guidance: Before posting or reacting online, take a moment to pray. Seek God's wisdom in your interactions and content consumption.

The world of social media is vast and ever-evolving. While it offers unparalleled opportunities for connection and expression, it's crucial for young Christians to approach it with discernment and wisdom. By setting clear boundaries, staying rooted in the Word, and continuously seeking God's guidance, you can navigate the digital realm in a manner that not only safeguards your mental and spiritual well-being but also glorifies God. Remember, in this digital age, it's not about abstaining but about engaging with purpose and prudence.

SECTION 7 Surviving My Health

THE OUTSIDER 43 How Can I Overcome My Depression?

Depression is a term often thrown around casually, but it is a severe mental health condition that can grip individuals, altering their perception, feelings, and daily functioning. In the formative years of 12-25, many factors like hormonal changes, societal pressures, academic expectations, and personal relationships can exacerbate feelings of sadness, leading to depression. As a young Christian, it's essential to understand that while faith provides solace and strength, addressing depression often requires a multifaceted approach.

Understanding Depression

Symptoms: Depression is more than just feeling sad. It manifests in various ways, including:

- Persistent feelings of sadness, hopelessness, or emptiness
- Loss of interest in activities previously enjoyed
- Fatigue or decreased energy
- Difficulty concentrating, remembering, or making decisions
- Changes in appetite or unintended weight changes
- Sleep disturbances
- Thoughts of death or suicide

Causes: Depression can arise from a combination of genetic, biological, environmental, and psychological factors. Events such as trauma, loss of a loved one, a difficult relationship, or any stressful situation can also trigger it.

A Christian Perspective: Depression doesn't imply a lack of faith. Many devout believers, including biblical figures like King David and the prophet Elijah, exhibited symptoms consistent with depression. Remember, having depression isn't a sign of spiritual failure.

Steps to Overcoming Depression

Acknowledge the Issue: The first step is acceptance. Denying or suppressing your feelings can lead to further emotional complications. Remember the words in Psalm 34:18, "Jehovah is near to the brokenhearted; He saves those crushed in spirit."

Seek Professional Help: There's no shame in seeking help. A therapist or counselor, especially one with a Christian background, can offer guidance, coping techniques, and even medication if deemed necessary.

Stay Connected: Isolation can intensify feelings of depression. Engage with your church community, join a support group, or simply talk to trusted friends and family. Share your feelings and let them offer comfort.

Dive into Scripture: Scripture is a source of hope and encouragement. Verses like Psalm 42:11, "Why are you cast down, O my soul?... Hope in God; for I shall again praise him, my salvation and my God," can offer solace.

Prayer: While prayer isn't a substitute for medical treatment, it's a powerful tool to combat feelings of despair. Regularly pouring out your heart to God can be therapeutic.

Establish a Routine: A consistent daily routine can provide structure and a sense of purpose. Whether it's daily Scripture reading, a walk, or simply tidying up, these activities can instill a sense of accomplishment.

Avoid Alcohol and Drugs: These might seem like quick fixes but can exacerbate depression and decrease the effectiveness of antidepressant medications.

Stay Active: Physical activity releases endorphins, which are natural mood lifters. You don't need to run a marathon, but regular walks, stretching, or any form of exercise can help.

Limit Stress: If possible, try relaxation techniques such as deep-breathing exercises, meditation, or journaling. Remember, it's okay to seek peace and prioritize self-care.

Set Boundaries: Avoid overcommitting or taking on too many responsibilities. It's crucial to recognize your limits and communicate them to others.

Refrain from Making Major Decisions: Depression can cloud judgment. If possible, delay major decisions until your mood improves or discuss them with trusted advisors or family.

Limit Negativity: Minimize exposure to negative influences and negative self-talk. Surround yourself with positive affirmations and people.

Consider Dietary Changes: Some evidence suggests that foods with omega-3 fatty acids (like salmon and tuna) and folic acid (like spinach and avocado) might help ease depression.

Remember, It's a Process: Overcoming depression isn't an overnight journey. Celebrate small victories and understand that there might be setbacks. Rely on your faith, knowing that "He gives power to the faint, and to him who has no might he increases strength" (Isaiah 40:29).

In the throes of depression, it might seem like the darkness won't lift. But, with the right tools, support, and spiritual guidance, the journey towards the light becomes more accessible. Embrace the love and strength that comes from God, lean on your support system, and remember: there's no shame in seeking help. Your journey might be challenging, but through perseverance, faith, and professional guidance, you can find the path to healing and peace.

THE OUTSIDER 44 How Can I Overcome My Anxiety?

Anxiety is a pervasive emotion, especially in the tumultuous years of adolescence and young adulthood. For young people between 12-25, this emotion can be heightened by myriad factors, from academic pressures to social dynamics, from personal relationships to future uncertainties. As a young Christian, understanding and managing anxiety becomes pivotal, especially when seeking to align one's life with God's word and purpose. Navigating anxiety is not about suppressing it but learning to cope, manage, and eventually thrive.

Understanding Anxiety

Defining Anxiety: Anxiety is more than just feeling nervous or worried. When these feelings persist, become overwhelming, and interfere with daily life, they might be indicative of an anxiety disorder.

Symptoms:

- Restlessness or feeling on edge
- Becoming easily fatigued
- Difficulty concentrating or mind going blank
- Irritability
- Muscle tension
- Sleep disturbances

Causes: Anxiety can be the result of a combination of factors, including genetics, brain chemistry, personality, and life events. For young individuals, external pressures such as academic stress, peer pressures, and societal expectations can exacerbate these feelings.

A Christian Perspective: It's important to recognize that experiencing anxiety does not indicate a lack of faith or trust in God.

Even the Apostle Paul admitted to feeling anxious about the churches he planted (2 Corinthians 11:28). What's crucial is how you address and manage these feelings in light of your faith.

Strategies for Overcoming Anxiety

Acknowledge the Feeling: Avoiding or denying your anxiety can amplify it. Recognize it, accept it, and remember Philippians 4:6-7, "Do not be anxious about anything, but in every situation, by prayer and petition, with thanksgiving, present your requests to God. And the peace of God, which transcends all understanding, will guard your hearts and your minds in Christ Jesus."

Engage in Prayer and Meditation: Regularly communicate with God. Share your worries and seek His peace. Meditation on Scripture can also be calming, grounding you in eternal truths amidst transient anxieties.

Seek Professional Guidance: A therapist or counselor can provide cognitive-behavioral strategies to manage and reduce anxiety. Opting for a Christian counselor can also ensure that the guidance you receive aligns with your faith.

Limit Stimulants: Reduce or eliminate the consumption of caffeine and sugar, as these can trigger or worsen anxiety.

Stay Active: Engage in regular physical activity. Exercise can help reduce anxiety and improve mood by releasing endorphins, the body's natural painkillers and mood elevators.

Rest and Sleep: Ensure you're getting adequate sleep. Establishing a regular sleep pattern can significantly impact your mood and energy levels.

Stay Connected: Regular fellowship with believers can provide a spiritual and emotional support system. Sharing your struggles with a trusted friend or mentor can be liberating.

Limit Exposure to Stressors: If watching the news or certain activities increase your anxiety, limit your exposure. Instead, engage in activities that promote peace and calm.

Set Realistic Goals: Set achievable tasks for yourself and celebrate your accomplishments. Breaking tasks into manageable chunks can make them less daunting.

Stay Informed: Understanding what triggers your anxiety can help in managing it. Keeping a journal can help identify patterns and triggers.

Grounding Techniques: Techniques such as the "5-4-3-2-1" method, where you identify five things you can see, four you can touch, three you can hear, two you can smell, and one you can taste, can help center you in moments of heightened anxiety.

Focus on the Present: Jesus said in Matthew 6:34, "Therefore do not be anxious about tomorrow, for tomorrow will be anxious for itself. Sufficient for the day is its own trouble." It's a call to focus on the present and trust God with our future.

In the journey of life, anxiety can sometimes feel like a constant companion, especially in our fast-paced, expectation-laden world. But with the right coping mechanisms, rooted in faith and complemented by professional guidance, it is possible to navigate through it. The road might seem challenging, but always remember: You're not alone in this journey. God is with you every step of the way, offering His peace, which surpasses all understanding.

Edward D. Andrews

THE OUTSIDER 45 How Can I Cope with This Constant Sadness?

The experience of persistent sadness can feel isolating and overwhelming, especially for young people navigating the volatile emotions of adolescence and early adulthood. Such emotions can be deeply entrenched, influencing every facet of one's life. But even in the depths of despair, there's hope, strength, and guidance to be found, particularly through a Christian perspective that promises healing, love, and understanding.

Understanding Persistent Sadness

Defining the Emotion: While everyone feels sad or down from time to time, constant sadness, especially when it lasts for more than two weeks and affects daily functioning, can be indicative of a deeper issue, like depression.

Symptoms:

- Feelings of hopelessness or pessimism
- Loss of interest in hobbies or activities
- Fatigue or decreased energy
- Difficulty concentrating or making decisions
- Sleep disturbances
- Appetite or weight changes
- Thoughts of death or suicide

Possible Causes: The origins of persistent sadness can be multifaceted, encompassing genetic factors, chemical imbalances in the brain, trauma, loss, or significant life changes.

A Christian Perspective: Experiencing such emotions isn't indicative of a lack of faith or God's abandonment. Remember Psalm 34:18: "The Lord is near to the brokenhearted and saves the crushed in spirit." God walks beside us, especially during our darkest moments.

Pathways to Coping and Healing

Connect with God: Foster an intimate relationship with Him through prayer, Scripture, and worship. By leaning into God's promises and seeking His presence, one can find solace and hope.

Scriptural Comfort: Meditate on scriptures that address sadness and despair. For instance, Psalm 42:11 says, "Why, my soul, are you downcast? Why so disturbed within me? Put your hope in God, for I will yet praise him, my Savior and my God."

Seek Professional Help: It's crucial to consult with a therapist or counselor, especially when sadness hampers daily functioning. Christian counseling can be particularly helpful in providing spiritual and therapeutic solutions.

Engage in Community: Isolation can exacerbate feelings of sadness. Surrounding oneself with a loving community, like a church or support group, can offer encouragement and a sense of belonging.

Healthy Lifestyle Choices: Engage in regular physical activity, maintain a balanced diet, and get adequate rest. These can play a pivotal role in emotional well-being.

Set Small Goals: Breaking tasks into manageable steps and setting priorities can alleviate feelings of being overwhelmed. Celebrate small victories, for they contribute to a greater sense of accomplishment.

Limit Stress: If possible, avoid known stressors. Explore relaxation techniques such as deep breathing, meditation, and journaling to handle stress.

Limit Alcohol and Avoid Drugs: These can make sadness worse and decrease the efficacy of antidepressant medicines.

Avoid Making Important Decisions When Down: Your perspective is skewed when in the throes of deep sadness. Give yourself time and seek guidance before making significant decisions.

Establish Routine: Maintaining a routine can offer a feeling of normality. Even simple things like setting specific mealtimes or allocating time for reading can make a difference.

Limit Negativity: Reduce exposure to negative influences and negative self-talk. Surrounding oneself with positivity, whether it's in the form of uplifting music, books, or company, can influence mood.

Stay Connected: Even a brief chat with a loved one can make a difference. Share your feelings and concerns, letting others in can be healing.

Remember God's Love and Faithfulness: Despite feelings of despair, remember that God's love remains constant. Romans 8:38-39 assures us that nothing "will be able to separate us from the love of God that is in Christ Jesus our Lord."

For young Christians experiencing constant sadness, the journey can be harrowing. Yet, with faith, support, and appropriate interventions, there's a way forward. No darkness is so profound that it can quench the enduring light of God's love and promise. Seeking help, whether divine, professional, or communal, isn't a sign of weakness, but of strength and self-awareness. It's a testament to one's commitment to healing, growth, and a life that honors God.

THE OUTSIDER 46
Protecting Children from Woke Ideological Education: A Biblical Perspective

This chapter provides biblical and practical insights for parents concerned about woke ideological education infiltrating schools. From fostering open communication and biblical foundations to exploring alternative education options, learn how to safeguard your children's minds and hearts.

Worried about the influence of woke ideology in your children's education? Gain a biblical perspective on protecting your children from such indoctrination. This article offers practical steps, grounded in Scripture, to help parents vigilantly monitor and guide their children's educational experience.

In today's complex social climate, parents face unprecedented challenges in raising their children according to the timeless principles of Scripture. Among these challenges is the incursion of "woke" ideological education into the school system, pushing agendas like critical race theory, gender ideology, and various forms of liberalism. These teachings stand in stark contrast to a biblical worldview. Let's explore how Christian parents can navigate this tricky landscape to protect their children.

Know What Your Children Are Learning

Key Scripture: Proverbs 22:6

"Train up a child in the way he should go; even when he is old he will not depart from it."

Core Principle: Parents should be actively involved in what their children are being taught. They should not hesitate to scrutinize lesson plans, textbooks, and school communication.

Counter-Educate with Scriptural Principles

Key Scripture: Ephesians 6:4

"Fathers, do not provoke your children to anger, but bring them up in the discipline and instruction of the Lord."

Core Principle: Counteract any unbiblical teachings with a strong foundation of biblical principles at home. Make the Bible and its teachings a regular part of your family life.

Be Aware of Subtle Influences

Key Scripture: 2 Corinthians 11:14-15

"And no wonder, for even Satan disguises himself as an angel of light. So it is no surprise if his servants, also, disguise themselves as servants of righteousness."

Core Principle: The danger often lies not in overt teachings but in subtle insinuations and activities designed to manipulate children's perceptions of self and reality, like the case of Jenny mentioned in your scenario.

Engage with Teachers and School Officials

Key Scripture: Matthew 10:16

"Behold, I am sending you out as sheep in the midst of wolves, so be wise as serpents and innocent as doves."

Core Principle: Maintain an active relationship with the teachers and staff at your child's school. Politely but firmly express any concerns you have about the ideological content of the education they are providing.

Consider Alternative Education Options

Key Scripture: Romans 12:2

"Do not be conformed to this world, but be transformed by the renewal of your mind, that by testing you may discern what is the will of God, what is good and acceptable and perfect."

Core Principle: Depending on the severity of the ideological indoctrination, parents may need to consider alternative educational options such as homeschooling or Christian schools that align with biblical values.

Legal Recourse and Civil Disobedience

Key Scripture: Acts 5:29

"But Peter and the apostles answered, 'We must obey God rather than men.'"

Core Principle: As last resorts, legal action or even civil disobedience may be necessary to protect your children. In the given case of Jenny, the parents had every biblical and moral right to protect their child from a dangerous and life-altering ideology.

Emotional and Spiritual Support

Key Scripture: 1 Thessalonians 5:11

"Therefore encourage one another and build one another up, just as you are doing."

Core Principle: Even when you take all the right steps, your child may still be influenced by destructive ideologies. Provide a strong emotional and spiritual support system at home, grounded in the love and teachings of Christ.

The Bible offers wisdom for every situation, including the modern challenges posed by ideological education contrary to biblical principles. Parents need to be vigilant, proactive, and rooted in the Word of God to effectively shield their children from these harmful influences. In extreme cases, like that of Jenny, the consequences of inaction can be devastating, altering a child's life in unimaginable ways. Therefore, it is imperative that parents take this stewardship seriously, trusting in God for wisdom and guidance.

The Reckoning of Jennifer: A Journey from Jenny to Johnny and Back Again

The Genesis of Confusion

It was a bright September morning when five-year-old Jenny crossed the threshold of Mrs. Winterton's kindergarten class. Mrs. Winterton, a staunch advocate for progressive ideologies, noticed Jenny playing with toy trucks. This, in her mind, was the *opportunity*—to mold and guide, though some would say manipulate, a young soul into a narrative deeply disconnected from Jenny's Christian upbringing.

"Jenny," Mrs. Winterton leaned down and whispered, "have you ever felt like you're really a boy inside? Remember, this is our little secret."

Over the next six years, a concerted, cultish effort unfolded within the school to steer Jenny away from her God-given identity. Worksheets, discussions, and counseling sessions were strategically employed to imprint upon Jenny that she was born into the wrong body.

When Hormones Speak Louder Than Words

At the vulnerable age of 12, the school initiated hormone therapy for Jenny, now going by Johnny. This chemical intervention marked her body and psyche in irreversible ways. Her voice deepened; body hair sprouted where it had never been.

The school finally decided to inform Jenny's parents—staunch, God-fearing Christians—of the "transformation."

"Jenny is now Johnny, and he's been undergoing hormone therapy for a while now," announced the principal. "We're also preparing for gender-reassignment surgery in two years."

Faith Versus System

"Absolutely not," Jenny's mother broke down in tears, clutching a Bible to her chest. "You are trying to destroy God's creation!"

"This is child abuse!" the father roared. "Jenny is a girl, created in the image of God!"

But their pleas fell on deaf ears. Labeling them as abusers, the school took them to court and won. Jenny was taken from her home and, at 14, underwent the irreversible surgery that detached her not just from her biological reality but also from her spiritual heritage.

Awakening

A decade passed. At 24, Jenny—living as Johnny—stumbled upon a Bible that had lain forgotten in her apartment. The words of Genesis leapt off the pages: "So God created man in his own image, in the image of God he created him; male and female he created them" (Genesis 1:27).

Her eyes swelled with tears. The years of ideological programming began to crumble. She realized she had been living a fabricated life, a distortion of the beautiful reality God had intended for her.

The Cost of Truth

Jenny's life turned into a cascade of psychiatric consultations and de-transition procedures. Yet, she was shattered to discover the irreversible havoc the hormone therapies had wrought—she would never bear children.

In a reckoning moment, Jenny took legal action against the school for grooming her into a life that robbed her of her most fundamental identity. After a tumultuous battle, the court ruled in her favor, awarding her three million dollars.

But what is the worth of three million dollars when your very essence has been stolen, manipulated, and destroyed?

Redeeming the Broken Pieces

Today, Jennifer lives a life of advocacy, warning parents and schools of the irreversible damage that ideological indoctrination can cause. While money can never replace what was stolen from her, her story serves as a cautionary tale—one of a life nearly ruined by a narrative that contradicted the fundamental biblical truths she had once held dear.

The words of Scripture that once comforted her family now provided her solace and a sense of mission: "Train up a child in the way he should go; even when he is old he will not depart from it" (Proverbs 22:6).

Though Jennifer cannot regain her lost years or her ability to bear children, she's found a renewed sense of purpose: to protect innocent lives from being ensnared by ideologies that defy God's beautiful design for human sexuality and identity.

The Inextinguishable Light

Jennifer found solace in her faith, finding her identity not in a cultural narrative but in her Creator. Her story, both heartbreaking and redeeming, serves as a stark reminder that when human designs conflict with Divine plans, the soul will inevitably yearn for the truth—a truth that can only be found in the sacred words of Scripture and the eternal love of God.

And so, Jennifer stands, a broken vessel, yet one that reflects the light of undeniable, Scriptural truth—a light that no amount of darkness can extinguish.

Preventative Measures for Protecting Children from Ideological Indoctrination

Open Communication Channels

First and foremost, parents must establish open lines of communication with their children. This means not merely talking *at* them but talking *with* them. "Train up a child in the way he should go; even when he is old he will not depart from it" (Proverbs 22:6). This training is a two-way street. Children should feel comfortable coming to their parents with any questions or concerns.

Vigilant Oversight of Educational Content

Parents should be vigilant in understanding what their children are being taught at school. This means reviewing textbooks, talking to teachers, and even sitting in classes if possible. If a curriculum is found to include elements contrary to biblical teachings, parents have a responsibility to take action—whether that means meeting with teachers, talking to administrators, or moving their child to a different educational setting.

Foster a Strong Biblical Foundation

Children should have a robust understanding of biblical principles from an early age. Daily family devotions, Scripture memorization, and candid discussions about biblical viewpoints on contemporary issues can lay a strong foundation. The Bible says, "These commandments that I give you today are to be on your hearts. Impress them on your children. Talk about them when you sit at home and when you walk along the road, when you lie down and when you get up" (Deuteronomy 6:6-7).

Teach Critical Thinking Skills

Teach your children not only *what* to think but *how* to think. This involves equipping them to assess an argument critically, to discern logical inconsistencies, and to identify manipulative tactics. Children who can think critically are less likely to be swept away by persuasive but flawed arguments.

Social Media and Peer Monitoring

Parents must be aware of not only what their children are being taught but also who they are associating with. Social media platforms are a hotbed for all kinds of ideologies. Ensure that your children understand the perils and pitfalls of using such platforms and monitor their usage.

Parental Involvement in School Activities

Being actively involved in school events and committees allows parents to be part of shaping the school environment. It also enables them to know what ideological issues may be infiltrating the school setting.

Legal Recourse and Rights

Know your rights as a parent. When you disagree with a teacher's or school's ideological stance that contradicts biblical truths, it's essential to understand the legal protections available to you. Engage with legal organizations committed to protecting religious freedom if you encounter challenges.

Strong Support Systems

Cultivate a strong support system composed of like-minded families, your church community, and possibly even legal experts who can offer advice. The saying, "It takes a village to raise a child," has a grain of truth. A strong, biblically-minded community can offer invaluable support in standing against ideological indoctrination.

Alternatives to Public Education

Consider alternative education options like homeschooling or Christian schools that align with your biblical beliefs. "Do not be yoked together with unbelievers. For what do righteousness and wickedness have in common? Or what fellowship can light have with darkness?" (2 Corinthians 6:14).

Being proactive, vigilant, and biblically grounded are the keys to safeguarding your children from destructive ideological influences. These measures are not guarantees, but they significantly reduce the risk of your children falling prey to harmful ideologies. Your home must become a sanctuary of biblical truth in a world increasingly hostile to such values. By fortifying this sanctuary, you're doing your God-given duty to protect and nurture the souls entrusted to your care.

The Exposure to Distorted Information on Sexual Matters at School

Today's educational landscape is fraught with pitfalls for young minds, especially when it comes to sexual education. Some schools, under the guise of being "progressive" or "inclusive," introduce sex education curriculums that promote ideologies contrary to Biblical principles. These can range from normalizing premarital sex to encouraging exploratory sexual behavior from an early age. Such distortions are often presented as "facts," leaving children confused and vulnerable. The Apostle Paul warned against such distortions, stating, "Let no one deceive you with empty words" (Ephesians 5:6).

Countering Sexual Misinformation

The best way to counteract sexual misinformation is through *clear, honest, and Biblical communication.* Parents should be the primary educators when it comes to sexual matters. By instilling a Biblical view of sexuality from a young age, children will be better equipped to discern falsehoods. Proverbs 22:6 says, "Train up a child in the way he should go; even when he is old he will not depart from it." Knowing the truth helps children recognize lies. Moreover, parents should stay informed about the curriculum taught at their child's school and, if necessary, seek alternative educational options that align with a Biblical worldview.

Biblical Insights on Sexual Matters

The Bible has much to say about sexual matters, presenting them within the context of marital commitment and mutual love. 1 Corinthians 7:2-3 advises, "But because of the temptation to sexual immorality, each man should have his own wife and each woman her own husband. The husband should give to his wife her conjugal rights, and likewise the wife to her husband." Hebrews 13:4 further emphasizes the sanctity of marital relations: "Let marriage be held in honor among all, and let the marriage bed be undefiled." The Bible clearly delineates sexual boundaries, emphasizing purity, fidelity, and the sacredness of the marriage covenant.

No Correlation Between Godly Knowledge and Immorality

Contrary to the notion that talking about sex will lead to sexual activity, *Biblically-grounded sexual education can serve as a protective measure.* When children understand the God-ordained purpose and boundaries of sexual relations, they are less likely to engage in immoral behavior. The Apostle Paul encouraged believers to "abstain from sexual immorality" and to "know how to control your own body in holiness and honor" (1 Thessalonians 4:3-4). Information grounded in God's Word serves to guide rather than tempt.

Progressive Education on Intimate Matters

Children should be taught about sexual matters progressively, in a manner appropriate to their age and level of understanding. Just as you wouldn't teach advanced calculus to a first-grader, there are appropriate times and ways to introduce various aspects of sexuality. The key is to be attentive and open, answering questions and providing guidance as the child matures. This can be likened to how Jesus tailored His teachings to His audience's level of spiritual maturity, stating in John 16:12, "I still have many things to say to you, but you cannot bear them now."

To conclude, we live in a world increasingly indifferent or even hostile to Biblical principles, especially regarding sexuality. It's imperative for parents to be vigilant, proactive, and grounded in the Word of God to guide their children effectively through the maze of sexual misinformation.

THE OUTSIDER 47 Help for Those Who Are Struggling with Transgender Ideology?

This chapter offers a range of questions and biblical counsel to help individuals grappling with transgender ideology. Discover how compassion and biblical truth can guide you back to God's intended design for your life as male or female.

In today's culture, issues surrounding transgender ideology have become increasingly complex and polarizing. The role of a Christian counselor is to approach these issues with both biblical fidelity and compassionate understanding. When counseling those struggling with transgender ideology, it's crucial to pose thoughtful questions that encourage self-examination while also providing biblical perspectives that offer clarity and hope.

Questions for Self-Examination

1. **Do you understand your intrinsic value as created by God?**
    - Scripture tells us that everyone is made in the image of God (Genesis 1:27). How does this biblical truth influence your understanding of your worth? [More on this below]

2. **What is your ultimate source of identity?**
    - Are you seeking your identity in your gender or in Christ? According to the New Testament, our identity should be in Christ (Galatians 3:26-29).

3. **What fears or concerns do you have about conforming to biological gender norms?**

- What does it mean for you to be a man or a woman, and how does that align with or contradict God's design in Scripture?

4. **Have you considered the long-term implications?**
   - Physical alterations like hormone therapy or surgeries have long-lasting consequences. Have you considered what God's Word says about our bodies being temples of the Holy Spirit (1 Corinthians 6:19-20)?

5. **Are you experiencing a form of suffering or distress?**
   - Is this issue of transgender ideology linked to a particular form of suffering or distress in your life? How does Scripture guide us in dealing with suffering (Romans 5:3-5)?

6. **What are your beliefs about God's design for gender and sexuality?**
   - Do your beliefs align with the biblical teaching that God created man and woman (Genesis 5:2), and that this creation has particular roles and functions (Ephesians 5:22-33)?

7. **How are you engaging with community?**
   - Are you isolating yourself or are you seeking wisdom from a community that aligns with biblical principles? (Proverbs 11:14)

8. **Have you prayed about this struggle?**
   - Prayer is our primary means of communication with God. Have you sought God's wisdom and guidance concerning these feelings (James 1:5)?

Biblical Counseling Perspectives

1. **Reaffirm Human Dignity**

- Regardless of their struggles, everyone is created in God's image and therefore possesses intrinsic value. Show them love and respect as Christ loved us. [More on this below]

2. **Root Identity in Christ**
    - Encourage them to find their identity in Christ, not in gender. Highlight Scriptures that show our identity as children of God through faith in Christ (John 1:12; Galatians 3:26-29).

3. **Focus on God's Design**
    - Remind them that God, as the Designer of all creation, designed the concept of male and female* with specific intentions (Genesis 1:27). Discomfort with one's biological sex is an indication that something is amiss, and the solution is not necessarily altering one's body but seeking alignment with God's design.

4. **Long-Term Implications**
    - Discuss the long-lasting medical, emotional, and spiritual ramifications of transitioning. Instead, suggest that they focus on becoming the man or woman that God created them to be, embracing the biological sex He assigned them at birth.

5. **Engage with Community**
    - Encourage them to connect with a community that will support them in a biblical manner. This community could include pastors, mature Christian friends, or Christian counselors who can provide additional guidance.

6. **Commitment to Prayer**
    - Encourage consistent prayer for wisdom and for God's will to be done. Reiterate the importance of relying on God for understanding and guidance.

7. **Scripture for Encouragement**
   - Share Scriptures that speak to God's love, grace, and transforming power. Passages such as Romans 12:2 can be particularly comforting.

8. **No Instant Solutions**
   - Make it clear that neither you nor they have all the answers now and that it's a journey that will require ongoing reliance on God and His Word.

9. **Offer Hope**
   - Ultimately, the Gospel message is one of hope. Despite the struggles we face in this life, the hope of eternal life through Jesus Christ is always available to us.

It's crucial to guide those struggling with transgender ideology to the infallible truths found in Scripture while being sensitive to the emotional and psychological distress they may be experiencing. The objective is to offer biblical counsel that leads to genuine freedom in Christ.

Made In the Image of God

The foundational biblical teaching that humans are made in the image of God should not be misconstrued to suggest that God endorses or supports a departure from the biological categories of male and female* that He created. Scripture is clear on this matter: God made human beings male and female* (Genesis 1:27). There is no biblical support for the idea that a multitude of genders exists; rather, the binary nature of gender is affirmed consistently throughout Scripture.

Moreover, being made in the image of God is not an endorsement of our fallen desires or propensities. All humans have a proclivity toward sin, a point that is emphasized in Genesis 6:5 and 8:21, which state that human thoughts are inclined toward evil. Jeremiah 17:9 further drives home the idea that the human heart is inherently deceitful and wicked. So, if someone claims that their feelings toward the opposite gender are divinely ordained because they are made in God's image, that argument is not consistent with what Scripture teaches about our fallen nature.

Addressing the matter practically, we do indeed have a range of desires and inclinations that are out of step with God's design, such as the propensity for sexual addiction for some. However, the presence of these desires doesn't justify acting upon them. Instead, these are areas of our lives that require transformation and renewal, as you've rightly pointed out.

Paul's teachings offer substantial hope in this regard. We are endowed with a conscience that distinguishes right from wrong (Romans 2:14-15), and this moral compass needs to be cultivated and shaped by God's Word. A neglected or repeatedly violated conscience can grow "seared" or calloused (1 Timothy 4:2), no longer providing reliable moral guidance.

Paul strongly encourages believers to "put on the new self" (Ephesians 4:24; Colossians 3:10), which is the regenerated nature that aligns with God's will. We are also urged to adopt the mind of Christ (Philippians 2:5; 1 Corinthians 2:16; Romans 15:5), a transformation that comes through the renewing of our minds (Romans 12:2). As we immerse ourselves in Scripture and surround ourselves with godly influences, our thinking becomes increasingly aligned with God's will.

In the same vein, Paul also exhorts believers to gain control over their bodies, referred to as "vessels" in passages like 1 Thessalonians 4:4. This means exercising self-control, a fruit of the Spirit (Galatians 5:23), and ensuring our bodies are instruments for righteous acts and not sinful desires.

So, if someone is struggling with transgender ideology or other feelings contrary to God's design, the counsel remains the same: Work on renewing the mind and transforming the heart according to God's Word. Aligning oneself with God's designed order for gender is a part of the broader Christian call to live righteously and holistically, something achievable through the empowering grace of God and the renewing knowledge of His Word.

What is a Woman?

* In the current cultural conversation, the definitions of "woman," "sex," and "gender" have become points of contention. There is an increasing tendency to differentiate between "sex" and "gender," with the former being viewed as biological and the latter as a social construct subject to fluidity. While the categories of "sex" and "gender" are indeed recognized in various disciplines, it's crucial to address this subject from a biblical perspective to counter unbiblical and unbiological assertions.

According to Scripture, the terms "sex" and "gender" are not separate categories but are intrinsically connected. God created human beings as male and female, and this binary categorization is rooted in biology and affirmed in theology (Genesis 1:27; 5:2). There's no room in this biblical framework for a multitude of genders or for the separation of gender from one's biological sex. Consequently, being a "woman" is not a socially constructed role or a personal choice but is rooted in the design of God.

The Hebrew expression for "woman" is 'ish·shah', essentially meaning a "female man." This term can also be translated as "wife," reflecting the interrelatedness of roles and identity between men and women in both the family and broader societal structures. The Greek term gy·ne' holds a similar dual meaning, being translated both as "woman" and "wife." In both cases, the terms are relational but grounded in biology. They do not offer an abstract, socially constructed concept of womanhood that can be molded to fit individual preferences or societal changes.

Moreover, the attempt to decouple "gender" from biology on the grounds that gender roles and characteristics are "taught" does not align with the biblical teaching that male and female distinctions were designed by God and are part of the created order. While it's true that societies have norms and roles, these are not what fundamentally define men and women. In the biblical view, a woman is, by definition, an adult human female who has passed the age of puberty. Her identity as a woman is not a social construct but a biological and theological fact.

Indeed, gender roles, as described in Scripture, are relationally significant. They carry both equal worth and different responsibilities in the context of family and church life (Ephesians 5:22-33; 1 Timothy 2:11-15). However, these roles are not arbitrarily or culturally imposed but are derived from the created order.

Addressing the issue pastorally, those struggling with gender dysphoria or confusion should be approached with compassion, acknowledging the psychological and emotional complexities involved. Yet, compassion must be coupled with truth. It would not be truly loving to affirm someone in a self-perception that conflicts with their God-given biological and theological identity.

In summary, from a biblical perspective, a woman is an adult human female whose identity as a female is not a social construct but a divinely ordained reality. The current attempts to redefine or expand the categories of "sex" and "gender" are not compatible with biblical teaching. The challenge for the Church is to compassionately engage with those who experience confusion in this area while steadfastly upholding the truth of Scripture.

THE OUTSIDER 48 What Does the Bible Say About Transgenderism and Cross-Dressing?

Some have shied away from using Old Testament Bible verses to talk about how we are to live our Christian life. They might say, "but some things in the Old Covenant Law were only for Israel." Or they might say, "Christians are not under the Mosaic Law." This is somewhat true, Christians are not under the Mosaic Law, but God does not change when it comes to moral values. How he felt then is how he feels now. Christians are not obligated to keep the ceremonial aspect of the Mosaic Law, but they are obligated to live by the principles of the Old Testament.

For example, Deuteronomy 22:5 is a verse in the Bible that says, "A woman shall not wear a man's garment, nor shall a man put on a woman's cloak, for whoever does these things is an abomination to the Lord your God." This verse is not discussing *styles* of clothing. The prohibition is regarding one's wearing on things specifically designed for the opposite sex. This verse is often interpreted as a prohibition against cross-dressing or wearing clothing that is traditionally associated with the opposite gender. It is believed to be part of a larger set of rules and regulations that were given to the Israelites by God through Moses, and it is considered to be a part of God's moral code for the Israelites. The verse is often understood to be a command for men and women to adhere to traditional gender roles and to dress in a way that is appropriate for their gender. It is also seen as a way to prevent confusion and maintain social order within the community.

When it comes to appearance and clothing, generally, a man wants to look like a man, and a woman wishes to look like a woman. For God's servant, be it an Israelite or a Christian, to behave contrary to this deep God-given sense of what is fitting would displease God. When Deuteronomy was written in the late 15th century BCE, men and women wore robes. However, there was a distinction between the clothing of men and women. The principle here in Deuteronomy 22:5 would not rule out a woman's wearing pants.

And it is true that Christians are not under the Mosaic Law. (Rom. 6:14) Insistence on applying the written form of a law or rule rather than its spirit or intent would be in opposition to Christian teaching. So, women wearing pants today would not be in opposition to the law, which was to prevent confusion about sexual identity and sexual abuse. While Christians are not under the Mosaic law, they are guided by its principles, which means using discernment, good judgment, and applying their conscience. The Bible's counsel is that women "women should adorn themselves in respectable apparel, with modesty and self-control, ... but with what is proper for women who profess godliness, with good works."—1 Tim. 2:9-10.

The Bible and Cross-Dressing and Transgenderism

The New Testament does not explicitly address the issue of cross-dressing or identifying oneself with words that denote members of the opposite sex or transgenderism. However, there are a few passages in the New Testament that could be interpreted as addressing these issues.

For example, in Deuteronomy 22:5, it is written: "A woman must not wear men's clothing, nor a man wear women's clothing, for the Lord your God detests anyone who does this." This verse could be understood as prohibiting cross-dressing.

In addition, 1 Corinthians 6:9 lists "effeminate" (malakoi in Greek) and "homosexuals" (arsenokoitai in Greek) among those who will not inherit the kingdom of God. The two Greek terms refer to passive men partners and active men partners in consensual homosexual acts. "nor men of passive homosexual acts [μαλακοὶ], nor men of active homosexual acts [ἀρσενοκοῖται]"

It is possible to interpret the passage in 2 Peter 2:10, which speaks of those who "indulge in the lust of defiling passion and despise authority," as applying to certain aspects of transgenderism.

In this verse, the author is warning against certain people who are indulging in sinful behaviors and showing contempt for authority. These people are described as bold and willful, and they do not show fear or respect when they speak against those who are held in high regard. The phrase "the lust of defiling passion" likely refers to sexual immorality or other forms of impurity, and the phrase "the glorious ones" could refer to angels or other beings of high status. Overall, the verse is cautioning against following the example of those who engage in sinful behaviors and disrespect authority, as such behavior is seen as sinful and disrespectful in the context of the Bible.

PREPARING YOUR APOLOGETICS BY KNOWING WHAT THEY MIGHT SAY

The New Testament does not directly address the issue of transgenderism, as the concept of gender identity and the experience of being transgender were not understood in the same way in the cultural context in which the New Testament was written. However, there are a few passages in the New Testament that those who support transgenderism might interpret as addressing issues related to gender and identity.

For example, in Galatians 3:28, it is written: "There is neither Jew nor Gentile, neither slave nor free, nor is there male and female, for you are all one in Christ Jesus." This verse, they would argue, suggests that in Christ, distinctions of gender, social status, and ethnicity are not important and that all people are equal. They would argue that this message of equality and inclusion could potentially be applied to the issue of transgenderism. Galatians 3:28 is a verse in the epistle to the Galatians, a letter written by the apostle Paul to a group of early Christian churches in the region of Galatia. The verse reads: "There is neither Jew nor Greek, there is neither slave nor free, there is no male and female, for you are all one in Christ Jesus." In this verse, Paul is emphasizing the unity and equality of believers in Christ. He is saying that in Christ, there is no distinction based on ethnicity (Jew or Greek), social status (slave or free), or gender (male or female). Instead, all believers in Christ are united and considered equal. This message of unity and equality is a central theme in the epistle to the Galatians, as Paul was addressing issues of division and conflict within the Christian community in Galatia. Overall, the verse is an important reminder that in the eyes of God, all believers in Christ are equal and united in their faith. It encourages believers to treat one another with respect and love, regardless of their background or circumstances. A believer in Christ is a person who has faith in Jesus Christ as their savior and follows his teachings. To be a believer in Christ, a person must repent of their sins and make a commitment to follow Jesus as their Lord and Savior. This involves turning away from a life of sin and seeking to live according to Jesus' teachings as recorded in the Bible.

Those who support transgenderism and cross-dressing would also argue that it is also important to remember that the overall message of the New Testament is one of love and acceptance of all people, regardless of their gender identity or expression. They would then twist the text Matthew 22:39, Jesus teaches that the second greatest commandment is to "love your neighbor as yourself." This message of love and compassion should be at the heart of how we approach the issue of transgenderism and other matters related to identity and diversity. The phrase "love your neighbor as yourself" is a summary of Jesus' teachings about how believers in him should treat others. It means that we should show the same love, care, and concern for others that we have for ourselves. This includes showing compassion, kindness, and respect to those around us and seeking to do good to others as we would want them to do good to us. The commandment to love our neighbor as ourselves is a call to love and serve others selflessly without seeking anything in return. It is an expression of the love and compassion that God has for his people and that he desires us to have for one another. This phrase "love your neighbor as yourself" does not refer to our accepting a person transitioning from one gender to another or cross-dressing.

You see, you have to anticipate these replies and then have a ready response.

The Bible presents gender as a binary (two genders), with people being referred to as either male or female. The rarity of intersex individuals does not undermine the Bible's creation design of man and woman. Rather, it gives another example of creation "groaning" because of all that has resulted from human imperfection.

Romans 8:20-22 Updated American Standard Version (UASV) [20] For the creation was subjected to futility, not willingly, but because of him who subjected it, in hope [21] that the creation itself also will be set free from its slavery to corruption into the freedom of the glory of the children of God. [22] For we know that the whole creation has been groaning together in the pains of childbirth until now.

God did not create those whose sex is ambiguous at birth. This is simply another example of the result of sin and missing the mark of human imperfection.

Those who truly wish to follow Christ means that they are to die to themselves (Matt. 16:24), they are to be transformed by the renewal of their mind, that by testing you may discern what the will of God is, what is good and acceptable and perfect (Rom. 12:2), and no longer walking as they once did (Eph. 4:17-18). The modern concept of being "true to ourselves" will always end in failure. Genesis 6:5 and 8:21 says that fallen man is mentally bent toward evil. Jeremiah 17:9 tells us that imperfect humans have an unknowable heart that is treacherous.

If the binary of male and female is God's creation, which is how he designed humans, and we are expected to accept it, then our biological distortions of his creation by our redefining terms to fit our preferences would be in opposition to God, displeasing to him. The Bible is quite clear that men should not act sexually as women (Lev. 18:22; Rom. 1:18-32; 1 Cor. 6:9-10), that men should not dress like women (Deut. 22:5), and that when men and women embrace, obviously other-gendered expressions of identity it is a disgrace (1 Cor. 11:14-15). We do not have an inalienable right to do whatever we want with our physical selves. We belong to God and should glorify him with our bodies (1 Cor. 6:19-20).

1 Corinthians 6:19-20 Updated American Standard Version (UASV)
¹⁹ Or do you not know that your body is a temple of the Holy Spirit within you, whom you have from God, and you are not your own? ²⁰ For you were bought at a price; therefore, glorify God with your body.

In this passage, the apostle Paul is writing to the Christian community in Corinth and reminding them that their bodies are not their own. They have been purchased by God through the death and resurrection of Jesus Christ, and therefore they belong to God. Paul is urging them to honor God by treating their bodies with respect and using them in ways that honor God. This includes taking care of their physical health and abstaining from behaviors that would harm their bodies, such as sexual immorality or substance abuse. It also includes using their bodies to serve others and to further God's kingdom.

THE OUTSIDER 49
GENDER IDENTITY:
Alternative Lifestyles—Does God Approve?

Gender Identity. The concept of identity popularized by Erikson (1959) is a description of eight stages of the life cycle during which we experience and express different styles of being a person. Identity combines the senses of who I am, what I do, and how I do it. The sense of identity may be inchoate, affective, and inarticulate in the young child, while the introspective adult may articulate precise descriptions of his or her identity. Gender identity is only a part of the whole sense of identity, yet at the same time it is a core component around which nongender aspects of identity are crystallized. Failure to achieve precise gender identity may impair the development of mature, complex adult identity, whereas the mature normal adult accepts gender identity as a given quality and elaborates other identity attributes.

Experience and Identity. Several aspects of personal experience must be identified and separated: the "me" experience, the "I" experience, and the "self" experience. Each is a part of the sense of identity but not necessarily gender-linked. The "me" experience refers to the sense of being alive, of possessing what happens to myself. Such experience is present probably in early infancy, later cognated upon, and then verbalized as the sense of me. The experience of me precedes and is distinct from the acquisition of sense of gender. The experience of "I" is the conscious appreciation of ego operations such as cognition, affect, and perception. That is, one experiences the sense of I am thinking, seeing, doing, feeling, deciding, acting. Again, the sense of I precedes and is distinct from the acquisition of sense of gender.

The term *ego* shall be construed operationally to describe mental operations—that is, cognition, perception, affect systems. Ego operations are experienced and directed. But ego operations are impersonal. We acquire different styles of ego operation that may become part of our identity formation, for example, "I am a fuzzy-thinking person" versus "I am a clear-thinking person." Ego styles are gender-linked. In a given culture males and females are differentially socialized in different styles of ego operations. We may say, for example, "You think like a woman" and thereby make an accurate observation of cultural influence on gender-linked ego style (Spence & Helmreich, 1978).

Self is the image of Who am I? It is a complex mental construction, including my ideal self or what I ought to be (the combined psychoanalytic ego ideal and superego), my desired self (a consciously constructed self-model), and my actual self (the observation of my person in action). Self-identity is neither innate nor epigenetic, as is true of me and I experiences. Rather, self-identity is learned, constructed, formulated, modified, and elaborated on throughout life (Gergen, 1971). Gender plays a major role in the development of self-identity. One can experience me, I, and ego operations apart from a sense of gender, but one does not experience self apart from a sense of gender.

It is obvious that sexual impulse, desire, and behavior are entwined with gender identity. Sigmund Freud interpreted sexuality as a basic determinant of identity. However, a century of research has demonstrated that sexuality is a reflection of gender identity rather than a determinant. That is, sexuality is acted out in terms of impulse, arousal, desire, and action on the basis of one's gender-identity formation (Stoller, 1968).

Anatomy and Destiny. A major question is raised by the obvious differences between male and female appearance, behavior, and role functions. Is this biological determinism or cultural artifact? It is appealing to assume that innate biological instincts account for male-female differences. In animal species we observe highly complex social behavior that is gender-linked. However, the biologic determinants of behavior shift with animal complexity; basic instincts are the same in human, monkey, pigeon, or worm. These generate drives, which become less directive as we ascend the phylogenic ladder, so that when we reach the level of humans, instinctual drive stimuli no longer determine specific behavioral complexes.

An example of this is the sexual instinct. The amoeba reproduces asexually at a predictable rate of fission. The earthworm has both male and female sex organs and copulates with another earthworm by matching male and female genitalia in random fashion. Frogs and birds mate only during a mating season, with gender-linked stereotyped courtship behavior and with a partner for the season. Higher mammals, such as the gorilla, form generational families, choose specific mates, mate during estrous seasons, and care for the young within the family structure. Young monkeys who are reared apart from the mother do not successfully copulate or care for their own young. In the human sexuality may never be expressed, in that celibate persons may live a normal and psychologically healthy life without significant sexual experience. Or persons may use sexual behavior to quell loneliness, anxiety, or conflict without experiencing any sexual pleasure. At the same time human sexual behavior is not necessarily linked to reproductive mating.

To conclude, in terms of biologic principles we cannot appeal to differences in male and female instincts to account for male-female variations in behavior per se.

The influence of genetic variation and hormonal influences on behavior must be considered. Persons with abnormal gender chromosomal patterns may exhibit genetic defects of deformations of skeleton or muscle formation. But their behavior may not differ from that of persons with normal gender chromosomes. If we administer sex hormones to a person, what will happen? In the average person, nothing. However, in some experiments, if one administers hormones to homosexual persons, they increase their homosexual activity level. That is, sex hormones increase the drive stimuli but do not change the sexual orientation of the person. Clearly then, gender behavior, including sexual behavior, cannot be accounted for primarily on biological grounds (Money & Musaph, 1977).

Facets of Gender Identity. The development of identity is biopsychosocial. We can truly speak of psychosexual identity, but more accurately we should speak of psychogender identity, since sexuality is an expression of gender sense. Eight variables contribute to psychogender identity (Money & Ehrhardt, 1972).

Variable 1: Chromosomal Gender. In the normal pattern the female has an XX sex chromosome pattern, the male an XY. In genetic abnormalities there may be five to six sex chromosome gene patterns, each giving rise to different clinical syndromes and involving different hormonal, musculoskeletal, and genital patterns and different levels of sexual potency. Yet a person with a female chromosome pattern may be born with male-appearing genitalia, be reared as male, and behave as male, and vice versa. The sex chromosome pattern obviously does not determine gender behavior.

Variable 2: Gonadal Gender. This refers to the presence of either testes or ovaries. In the embryo the human is bisexual, and under hormonal influence one set withers and the other grows. Yet in some cases of aberrant chromosomal and/or hormonal influence, the external genitalia may develop of one gender while the gonads are of opposite gender. Thus an infant may be born with female-looking genitals along with well-developed undescended testicles, or vice versa. Again, the primary gonads do not determine gender orientation or behavior.

Variable 3: Hormonal Gender. Males and females do have distinctive hormonal systems, produced by both the gonads and other body organs. Malfunction or disequilibrium in the hormonal systems may influence the male-female balance of hormones. In turn this may result in masculinization or feminization of body traits, such as voice, hair pattern, breast development, fat deposition, skeletal growth, and development of external genitalia in embryo. In children this may result in a chromosomal and gonadal male with a female hormone balance that causes feminization of body structure, or vice versa. Nonetheless, the person will act male or female in accord with that person's rearing, regardless of the hormonal balance or body habitus.

Variable 4: Internal Genitalia. This refers to the vagina and uterus in the female and prostate in the male. These internal organs develop in accord with embryonic hormonal patterns.

Variable 5: External Genitalia. These organs are the most visible evidence upon which we first assign gender. Yet they may be misleading. As noted, variations in chromosomal, gonadal, and hormonal variables may produce external genitalia that appear of one gender yet are opposite to all other previous gender variables. A male may not develop closure of the bilateral pubic genital tissues and appear to have a vulva. A female may have overdevelopment of the clitoris that looks like a penis. But the external genitalia do not determine gender identity.

In the case of transsexualism the person has the identity of one gender (I experience my identity as female) while having all the normal body attributes of the other gender (I live in a male body). In this instance the distinction between gender body attributes (biological) and gender identity (psychological) is clearly seen.

Variable 6: Gender of Assignment and Rearing. This refers to the label the parent gives the child as either male or female. Boys and girls are handled differently as infants by their parents. They are treated differently long before they can talk or cognate on their own gender identity. The child is socialized into a basic gender identity long before language acquisition. Such gender acquisition precedes language. The threshold for fixation of gender identity is about 18 months, while the point of no return for change in gender reassignment is about 30 months. After 4 years of age it is almost impossible to change gender assignment without severe psychological conflict in the child.

Variable 7: Core Gender Identity. This is the first basic sense of identity that is crystallized via cognition as part of self-identity. The child cognitively is able to state, I am a boy or girl. This appears to be organized as a cognitive construct between ages three or four. In contrast, the gender assignment has already been well established. It appears that when parents assign the child one gender (male) and treat the child as the other gender (female), the psychological conditions for transsexualism are created (I have been labeled a male but am treated as and expected to be a female). In psychotic regressive states we can observe similar confusion about core gender identity in patients who demonstrate no gender confusion in normal states. Persons with primitive character disorders similarly demonstrate gender identity confusion.

Variable 8: Gender Role Identity. This refers to the social patterns of appearance, behavior, and role performance associated with the sociocultural definitions of masculinity or femininity. There is probably some degree of psychological linkage between the sense of maleness or femaleness and behavior in masculine or feminine roles as defined by the culture. For example, in cultures with weak male roles the males demonstrate a higher incidence of identification with women, as in couvade (male pregnancy fantasies). One can experience a strong sense of maleness or femaleness, however, and not behave in traditional or expected gender-linked roles. For example, a feminine woman can be a police officer; a masculine man can knit doilies (Munroe & Munroe, 1977).

In the area of social gender roles there has been much confusion about the difference between gender identity and gender roles. The concept of androgyny has been promoted to do away with gender distinctions. This misses the point that gender identity is ineluctably a part of personal identity but that many social roles and behaviors need not be gender-linked (Sargent, 1977). The mature person with a secure gender identity is free to elaborate a wide variety of social role behaviors that become part of personal identity apart from gender.

Gender and Self-Identity. Although self-identity need not be tied to gender in many aspects, in another sense self-identity is always linked to gender. There are eight stages of psychological development of identity, according to Bemporad (1980). Each stage is not left behind but is incorporated into the next developmental level. Thus in the mature adult we continue to see reflections of each stage of identity.

Stage 1. In what is called an oral incorporative mode the newborn engulfs everything encountered. This style of relating to the world is to take it in and make it part of himself. The young infant does not differentiate between self and other. The lack of body boundaries, the timeless sense of fusion with the other, the experience of engulfing and being engulfed is reexperienced in adult life in sexual orgasm. The theme of incorporative identity is reflected in love play with nibbling or biting and in courtship with the primordial declaration: "I love you so much I could eat you up!"

Stage 2. Between 15 and 36 months the young child identifies the body as part of self, and body image becomes a major nidus of self-identity. Possession of body is possession of identity. The same motif is seen in adults who experience a sense of loss of identity when accident, surgery, or illness results in loss or immobilization of body parts. Where body is still a major source of self-identity and sexualized, the loss of genitalia (gonads, breasts) or sexual function may be experienced as a major loss of identity. The statement "I don't feel like a man or a woman anymore" reflects a sexualized fixation on body as a source of identity and of gender identity.

A bit later the child extends the body boundaries to objects, clothes, or playthings as body extensions. My things are my body, are part of me. Again, in adults we see identity rooted in possessions as a source of identity or gender identity reinforced through possessions: "I have a gun, ergo I am a male!" or "I have a house, ergo I am a woman!"

Stage 3. Between 3 and 5 the child differentiates self from other objects. There is generic identification with children of the same gender. Boys and girls reinforce gender identity by modeling and emulating behavior and social roles of the same-gender parent. Play helps the child to learn how to be an adult person. Identity is related to how one looks, acts, behaves. Playing house is modeling behavior that reinforces gender identity. Identity is developed in terms of social custom that differentiates men and women. Little girls cook, bake, and sew. Little boys pound nails and mow grass. This need not and should not be preparatory role behavior for adulthood, but some gender-linked role modeling is necessary to reinforce the sense of "I am becoming a man or a woman." This is identity through same-gender comparison.

Stage 4. Ages 5 to 7 is the oedipal period, in which identity development occurs through opposite-gender comparison. The child elaborates gender identity by modeling behavior of the same-gender parent with the opposite. The boy tries to behave with mother like father does. The girl treats father like mother does. Children will naturally emulate erotic and seductive behavior of the parent. Children act this way not because of infantile sexual strivings, as Freud suggested, but rather because they are modeling the sexy behavior of their parents. At this stage children need affirmation from both parents that these early strivings toward adult behavior are not bad and that in adulthood they will find mates to replicate the behavior of mother and father. Disapproval of either parent, fear of either parent, or failure to successfully identify with the parent of the same gender all lead to failure at this stage of identity development. In the view of some theorists, parents have, therefore, the potential to contribute to the development of a homosexual orientation. In such a view, homosexuality is not a problem of sexuality but a failure in maturation of identity development at the oedipal stage (Stoller, 1968).

Stage 5. In Latency, 7 to 12 years, the child elaborates personal identity via doing things. Skill acquisition enables the child to define personal abilities and ego coping style unique to him or her. Again, skill acquisition is in part linked to gender: learning male skills and female skills. But at this stage it is possible to also offer children androgynous skill acquisition not linked to gender but instead adding to development of unique individual skills and identity.

Stage 6. In adolescence the sense of self is heightened. Sexual drive stimuli are increased, and attraction to the opposite gender occurs. But what is the nature of the attraction? It is an exchange of mutual ideal images. The teenager falls in love with a projected image of an ideal, which is reciprocated. When the ideal image is tarnished by harsh reality, the puppy love dissolves. The attraction is reciprocated appreciation of an ideal self. When this is then eroticized, one feels a sexual attraction. Sexual interaction becomes a vehicle for reinforcement of self-identity.

Stage 7. In young adulthood a major transmutation of identity must occur from "what I do gives me identity" to "who I am gives meaning to what I do." That is, external attributes have given value to self-identity. Now the young adult must invest in internal attributes, an internal constructed sense of self, and identity apart from external exigencies. Failure to accomplish this task results in persons who seek others, sexually or not, to reinforce their own identity, self-esteem, value, and self-worth. So-called identity crises may occur in adults who lean on external definitions of identity and therefore lose their sense of self when those externalities diminish or disappear.

Stage 8. Mature adulthood involves the capacity to share one's identity with another. Mature love involves the capacity to retain one's own autonomy and identity but also acquire a shared identity with a partner. Marriage and sexuality can occur without sharing the intimacy of identity. Mature love involves "growing together" (Curtin, 1973). Here gender identity merges into a joint male-female identity of a marital pair.

The biblical observations that "male and female created he them" and "the two shall become one" represent the journey of psychogender development. The child begins with genderless fusion, acquires a gender identity, and moves on to an autonomous unique personal identity. But the mature adult shares gender identity with a mate of the opposite-gender identity in a new fusion that is a gender and sexual union, two unique self-identities, and a conjoint mutual marital identity. Thus there is the sense of paradox, in that identity is on the one hand profoundly rooted in a distinct sexual gender and on the other hand unites and transcends gender.

Edward D. Andrews

THE OUTSIDER 50 Finding Peace Amidst Chaos: A Guide for Today's Youth

Navigate the chaos of the modern world with our Christian guide for today's youth, exploring ways to find divine peace. Discover how a deep relationship with God, engaging in God's Word, active fellowship, and service can bring lasting tranquility in your life.

In today's world, where chaos and uncertainty seem to be the new normal, finding peace can often feel like a daunting task. The daily bombardment of disturbing news, the peer pressures of modern society, and the unique challenges that come with transitioning from childhood to adulthood can stir a whirlwind of emotions, confusion, and anxiety. However, as young Christians, we are not left without a guiding light and an anchor in these tumultuous times. Our faith in God and the timeless wisdom of His Word offers us the pathway to true peace amidst the chaos.

The Bible assures us in Philippians 4:7 that "the peace of God, which surpasses all understanding, will guard your hearts and your minds in Christ Jesus." This peace is not contingent on external circumstances but is anchored in the unwavering nature of God and His promises. So, how can you, as a young Christian, access and sustain this divine peace in a chaotic world?

Understanding God's Peace

To find God's peace, it's crucial to understand what it is and what it is not. God's peace does not necessarily mean the absence of problems or discomfort. Rather, it's an inner sense of calm, assurance, and trust in God, even amidst difficulties and chaos. It's the tranquility that stems from knowing God is in control and that He is working all things together for our good (Romans 8:28).

Cultivate a Deep Relationship with God

Building a deep, personal relationship with God is the cornerstone of finding His peace. This relationship begins with accepting Jesus Christ as your personal Lord and Savior, acknowledging your need for His grace, and deciding to follow His ways.

Prayer is a vital tool in building and sustaining this relationship. Philippians 4:6 urges us, "do not be anxious about anything, but in everything by prayer and supplication with thanksgiving let your requests be made known to God." Through consistent prayer, you cultivate open communication with God, share your worries, and receive His peace.

Immerse Yourself in God's Word

Reading and meditating on God's Word is an essential practice in finding peace. The Bible is a reservoir of God's promises, wisdom, and guidance. By studying it, you align your mind with God's thoughts, which results in peace. Verses such as John 16:33, where Jesus assures us that He has overcome the world, provide hope and peace during challenging times.

Foster Christian Fellowship

Surrounding yourself with other believers can help you maintain peace. Fellow Christians can offer support, encouragement, and spiritual insights that can fortify your peace. Participate actively in your local church, join Bible study groups, or engage in Christian youth organizations where you can grow together in faith.

Serve Others

Serving others in love is a powerful antidote to the chaos and self-centeredness of the world. Acts of service take our focus off our problems and allow us to experience the joy and peace of fulfilling God's commandment to love our neighbors (Mark 12:31).

Embrace God's Sovereignty

Realizing that God is in control, even when things seem chaotic, brings peace. Acknowledge His sovereignty in all situations and trust that He is capable of turning any situation around for your good.

Maintain a Lifestyle of Praise and Thanksgiving

Praise and thanksgiving keep our minds on God's goodness, thus fostering peace. Regularly express your gratitude for what God has done and continues to do in your life. Cultivate a heart of worship, praising God in songs and hymns.

Finding peace amidst chaos is a journey, not a one-time event. It requires an ongoing commitment to grow in your relationship with God, trust Him, and remain grounded in His Word. Remember, you're not walking this path alone; God has promised never to leave nor forsake you (Hebrews 13:5). Cling to Him, rely on His promises, and let His peace rule in your heart, regardless of the chaos around you.